RAISING THE FUTURE THE MONTESSORI WAY

BECOME A CONFIDENT, GENTLE PARENT RAISING AN EMPOWERED CHILD

BETHANY LOUISE

© **Copyright 2021 - All rights reserved.**

The content contained within this book may not be reproduced, duplicated or transmitted without direct written permission from the author or the publisher.

Under no circumstances will any blame or legal responsibility be held against the publisher, or author, for any damages, reparation, or monetary loss due to the information contained within this book, either directly or indirectly.

Legal Notice:

This book is copyright protected. It is only for personal use. You cannot amend, distribute, sell, use, quote or paraphrase any part, or the content within this book, without the consent of the author or publisher.

Disclaimer Notice:

Please note the information contained within this document is for educational and entertainment purposes only. All effort has been executed to present accurate, up to date, reliable, complete information. No warranties of any kind are declared or implied. Readers acknowledge that the author is not engaged in the rendering of legal, financial, medical or professional advice. The content within this book has been derived from various sources. Please consult a licensed professional before attempting any techniques outlined in this book.

By reading this document, the reader agrees that under no circumstances is the author responsible for any losses, direct or indirect, that are incurred as a result of the use of the information contained within this document, including, but not limited to, errors, omissions, or inaccuracies.

CONTENTS

Introduction   5

1. WHAT IS THE MONTESSORI APPROACH?   11
   Overview of Montessori   15
   Four Planes of Development   18
   Montessori Now   26

2. THE MONTESSORI APPROACH TO WEANING   28
   What to Feed Your Baby   30
   The Montessori Approach to Weaning   36
   Montessori Checklist   40

3. MONTESSORI APPROACH TO PLAY   43
   The Five Characteristics of Play   45
   What Is a Montessori Playroom?   48
   Montessori at Home   51
   Activity Ideas   53

4. THE MONTESSORI TOY GUIDE   63
   Five Characteristics of Montessori Toys   66

5. MONTESSORI APPROACH TO SLEEPING   75
   Montessori Bedroom Essentials   77
   Establishing a Routine   81
   Tips for Using a Floor Bed   83
   Babyproofing Your Home   86

6. MONTESSORI APPROACH TO POTTY TRAINING	91
Preparation—How and When to Start and What Equipment You'll Need	94
Montessori-Inspired Phrases	98
Tips to Remember	102
7. MONTESSORI APPROACH TO DISCIPLINE	104
Setting Limits	110
Tips for Montessori Discipline	113
Montessori Communication Tips	116
Staying Calm	117
8. KEY BENEFITS OF IMPLEMENTING THE MONTESSORI METHODS	125
Five Reasons to Choose Montessori	127
Five Reasons Why Montessori Methods Work	130
Benefits of a Montessori Preschool	132
Conclusion	137
References	143

INTRODUCTION

All parents want the same thing—for their children to be happy and healthy. Children are wonderful and curious beings with the ability to explore, adventure, and find their own way. In order for a child to become the best version of themselves, we must provide them with a nurturing and encouraging environment. We must pay attention to detail and allow ourselves to see our children as intelligent individuals with various abilities and talents that they are yet to explore. Every child is different, with different wants and needs, so it is necessary to treat every child as an individual, providing them with the opportunity to follow their own path, rather than a path that has been chosen for them. Allowing a child to make their own decisions opens up a world of curiosity and fun for them and can help them to achieve their own independence.

It can be incredibly overwhelming and scary bringing a baby into the world, especially for those who have no experience raising children. Having a baby for the first time is like entering unknown territory; you don't know what will happen next. Many people, including parents, friends, and family, can have expectations and advice that you may or may not want to follow. Sometimes it can feel as though everyone is telling you how to look after your baby. You may have also built up your expectations of how you will perform as a parent, and more often than not, the picture you had painted is nothing like the real thing. Adjusting to all the changes in your life alongside the never-ending feeling that you're not getting it right can leave you feeling incredibly alone and frustrated. You may look at other parents and think they're doing a better job than you are—causing you stress. You are not alone. Feeling this way is not uncommon. Most parents experience these feelings, and most parents struggle at first, and it is OK. If you are expecting a child or a new parent, this is a great time to learn new parenting techniques that will benefit your child and yourself.

If you are already a parent and you are experiencing a stressful home environment, you may feel like your children don't listen to you or that you are not in control. You may feel like you are constantly worrying about your child and don't know whether your current approach is working. As parents, our time is limited, and so is our energy. We don't only have to make decisions for ourselves anymore, but for our tiny humans and our families as a whole. We must find approaches to parenting that make life easier for both parents and children. You may feel like you have exhausted all avenues—but don't give up; the Montessori methods are here to help you and your child.

Whether you are a teacher, a babysitter, or a daycare worker, taking care of a group of children can be difficult. Each child is individual; therefore, traditional teaching methods may not always be successful, especially for younger children. The first years of a child's life will define their brain's development, social skills, and emotional abilities. As a teacher or someone responsible for a group of children, it is important to prioritize a child's individual needs rather than approach a group of children in the same way. Teaching a group of children can be very rewarding, but it can also be challenging and tiresome. We must practice patience and become as organized as possible, freeing up time to observe each child and recognize their abilities.

You may have heard of the Montessori approach but do not know how to implement this method into your life effectively. The Montessori way can be beneficial for not only children but teachers and parents too. Learning Montessori methods before you have a baby will allow you to prepare yourself for your child's education and well-being. The Montessori methods will allow you to build deeper relationships with your young children and build mutual respect between the parent and child. Montessori methods will help you become more organized, allowing you to invest more time and energy into your children.

Remove stress from your home environment and facilitate a child's learning healthily and independently, ultimately making life easier for yourself and your child. Create a warm, relaxed and comfortable environment for a group of children to learn alongside one another in their own way while enjoying themselves and building relationships. We sometimes underestimate what children are capable of, but we notice how much children can achieve by themselves when we use the Montessori approach. This book will cover all of the day-to-day challenges we face as parents and teachers.

There are many benefits to the Montessori way, but most importantly, giving a child the opportunity to educate themselves, learn from their surroundings, and thrive in a nurtured environment. Montessori children can become self-motivated, independent, and enthusiastic individuals with high self-esteem and good manners. They are more likely to have better social and problem-solving skills than children that have been taught and raised by traditional schooling and parenting methods. Raising a child with Montessori methods will ultimately help the child reach his or her full potential in all aspects of life.

This book will talk about Maria Montessori and her ideas, which developed into a well-known parenting and educational technique. We will discuss the Montessori approach, why it is beneficial to children's development, and how to implement the method into your child's life. We will go over important aspects of parenting, including significant milestones and how to approach them the Montessori way.

Since becoming a parent myself, I have studied many different parenting techniques and have become a specialist in gentle parenting styles. I have researched and practiced all methodologies of Montessori, and I apply these teachings in my day-to-day family life. I am passionate about Montessori as I have studied this parenting technique for five years and have successfully used this method on two of my children. From my own experience of the world of the unsettled toddler and parent power struggles, I would like to help others achieve a relaxed and stress-free family home environment.

With a first-class degree in language and psychology, alongside my experiences from the early years of parenting, I can assure you that I have approached this topic from a well-rounded and detailed perspective. This book is here to help you test various Montessori approaches across all elements of day-to-day life so that you can experience the benefits of a more calm and nurturing environment.

1

WHAT IS THE MONTESSORI APPROACH?

Montessori is an established style of education invented by Maria Montessori, one of the first female physicians in Italy. She dedicated her life to learning about children and bettering their education. The methods she implemented were to help children build independence and confidence within a natural environment. She traveled all over the world and inspired many people to follow her approach to educating children. Montessori methods are still popular to this day, and there are now hundreds of Montessori schools worldwide. Montessori was an educator and innovator who sparked a new way of raising and teaching children. Maria was born in Chiaravalle, Italy, in 1870 and then grew up in Rome. She was surrounded by libraries, museums, and good schools, and she took advantage of her environment. Her parents were intellectual people. Her mother was well-educated and an avid reader, which was a rarity in Italian women in that period. Her father was a financial manager. She had a great relationship with both of her parents, who encouraged her throughout her life.

Maria explored many subjects and studied vigorously before creating the Montessori methods. She was an exceptional student who didn't let traditional expectations for women hold her back. At age 13, Maria entered an all-boys technical institute with the hopes of pursuing an engineering career, which was an unusual aspiration for a young girl at that time. When she graduated at age 16, Maria made the decision to take on further education within the same institute. At age 20, Maria graduated with good grades—especially in mathematics and science. By this point, she had changed her mind about her career goals. Maria had instead decided that she wanted to become a doctor. She had to study vigorously to gain acceptance to medical school. When she first approached her medical studies, she was rejected from the University of Rome. However, she persevered and took on extra courses of study. She later obtained admittance to the school, opening doors for other women in this area. Maria graduated from medical school in 1896 as a doctor of medicine.

With her dedication, she defied expectations and helped contribute to paving the way for other women. Maria was interested in education after focusing on psychiatry in her early years of medical practice. She began to study pedagogy and educational theory. She observed the educational methods that were used to teach children with intellectual and developmental disabilities. She later raised debate over these methods, criticizing the effects they had on the children. In 1900, Maria became the codirector at a training institute for special education teachers. She used her time to observe teaching methods and analyzed what approach worked best. She applied these methods in her teachings, and the children made unexpected achievements—leading to Maria's methods being recognized as a success.

Maria opened the first Casa Dei Bambini in 1907, a childcare center in San Lorenzo. The center catered to underprivileged children aged 3 to 7. In the center, the adults left the children to their own devices while the parents went out to work. The methods that they used to take care of the children made for a high-quality learning environment. The children benefited considerably—they started to show interest in working with puzzles, learning how to prepare meals, and manipulating learning materials that Maria had designed. Maria would observe children and watch how they learned from their surroundings and the environment. She used her observation and experience to create learning materials that would help the children and designed the classroom in a way that allowed children access to all materials. The children were allowed to pick out their own materials and make independent decisions without having to ask for help.

The methods that Maria used in her program led the children to learn and thrive. They started to display natural self-discipline, concentration, and attention. Word began to spread about Montessori methods and reached the attention of leading educators and journalists. The method became extremely popular, and by 1910, Montessori schools were all over Western Europe and were starting to become established worldwide. In 1911, in Tarrytown, New York, the first Montessori school in the US was opened.

Maria spent the rest of her life learning about children and developing her approach to education. She showed effort in her work through her lectures, articles, and books. She created a program for other teachers so that they could understand and implement Montessori methods. Many teachers and parents worldwide have adopted Maria's approach to teaching and learning. Maria was an avid women's rights activist, and she raised discussion on the lack of opportunities for women; she was passionate about the subject and wrote about it frequently. In Italy and beyond, Maria was recognized as a fierce advocate for feminism. In 1940 there were disruptions between Italy and Great Britain; during this time, Maria had traveled to India lecturing her work. She had to remain in India for the remainder of the war. Maria used this time to train and educate teachers on the Montessori methods. After the war, she returned to Europe and spent her final years in Amsterdam, dying peacefully in 1952. Maria received recognition worldwide for her marvelous work and was nominated for three years in a row for the Nobel Peace Prize.

OVERVIEW OF MONTESSORI

Montessori education encourages critical thinking, organization, self-awareness, and a lifelong passion for learning. The Montessori way of learning allows a child to become the best version of themselves—without pressure, interruption, or coercion from others. Montessori schools are designed to give children a comfortable, secure, and favorable environment, helping them to discover themselves and their interests independently. Children are treated with respect and given the support they require to learn and thrive within their surroundings. The Montessori teacher pays attention to each child individually, which helps the teacher grow relationships with the children and learn their personal interests. The children are aware that they will receive support or help from their teacher if they need it—allowing them to build trust in their teacher and confidence within themselves.

In a Montessori environment, the surroundings are tidy and straightforward, with all items and materials strategically placed so that the children can easily find and make use of the provided learning materials. A Montessori classroom promotes the natural growth of relationships while developing social skills and respect for one another. The children find it easier to concentrate in an environment where they choose what they want to work with. The children have the opportunity to discover and explore their interests. They are not disrupted; instead, they are left to their own devices to learn and play. The children experience the freedom to find their place in the classroom and naturally build relationships with the other students.

The learning materials provided to the children give them the chance to explore and develop their cognitive abilities. The toys and materials are designed to help children figure out how to work them by themselves. Instead of helping the children, the adults observe them and allow them to think and act by themselves and make their own decisions. The adults gently guide the children instead of disciplining them and enable them to develop confidence and manners.

The Montessori environment is created to suit the height and size of a child, allowing them to reach items and access shelves, tables, and chairs so that they do not have to ask for help. The environment is neat and tidy, clean and appealing, with a sense of community. Children can sit in groups or alone, depending on where their instincts take them. Montessori classrooms are divided into separate areas, each with a different theme or topic, providing the children with the freedom to explore. Learning materials are displayed so that the children can easily examine them and choose if they want to make use of them. The environment encourages the children to be independent, allowing them to use their minds, realize their mistakes, and learn from their errors.

The classrooms consist of groups of children of mixed ages. The age groups are 0 to 3 years old, 3 to 6 years old, 6 to 9 years old, and 9 to 13 years old. The children benefit from the diversity of their ages and learn from one another, allowing them to experience relationships with children younger and older than themselves. Following and observing the children without disrupting them can allow the teacher or parent to recognize their needs and characteristics. It can be beneficial for teachers to determine each student's skill level, the child's emotional and physical state, and how they approach relationships and socialization. The close examination can help build an environment that suits each child and their individual wants and needs. Children are curious and need an environment where they can flourish and learn how to approach the world independently.

Children can use scientifically developed materials to develop their skills and intellectual abilities. These materials are formulated to accommodate the classroom and the children's interests, based on their age and current evolutionary stage. The materials are designed to help the children repeat their actions, making it easier for them to concentrate and understand their learning materials. The materials will allow the child to know whether they are using them correctly and ultimately notice their errors. The children will start to learn that mistakes are part of the learning process and that with each try, they improve their skills—this helps the children develop a positive attitude towards learning. Children gain self-confidence when they work out how to perform by themselves.

Children are more eager to learn when presented with opportunities that offer them an interesting or exciting purpose. A Montessori teacher will observe a child's wants and needs, interests, and capabilities. From these observations, the teacher will give the children guidance and offer them materials and ideas that align with their interests and abilities. Unless it is required, the teacher does not interrupt or intervene with the children. Instead, they allow the children to progress within their development freely. There are no rewards or punishments for the children, so they learn inner discipline, granting them satisfaction from their own work. Based on the child's level of development, the teacher will continue to observe the child and introduce new projects and ideas, either individual to the child or presented to a group of children at the same level. As the children advance, they will begin to organize their schedule and set new goals for themselves at the beginning of each week—the children are responsible for their own learning and development.

FOUR PLANES OF DEVELOPMENT

The Four Planes of Development is a concept that Maria Montessori created based on her developmental psychology views and research. This theory considered all aspects of a child's evolution, including emotional, academic, spiritual, and moral development. Children are born into a world full of opportunity and potential, and with the ideal environment and approach, a child can reach their full potential in all areas of life.

Traditional education methods involve teaching children as much information as possible until they reach maturity—continuously building on what they have previously been taught. Maria Montessori's ideas were different from traditional methods, as she believed that children learn in cycles. If children follow their natural learning process, they will learn and academically advance at their own pace while also developing spiritually, mentally, and emotionally.

The First Plane is from birth to age 6. The first three years of a child's life will determine their future development. In Montessori, they call this stage the "spiritual embryo"—when the child has finished their physical growth in the womb and has started their spiritual development in the world. Children grow and develop from the experiences of their environment, what they see and hear, and their relationships with others. Children are in discovery mode at this age—they absorb all of the information surrounding them and start to explore, interact, and learn from their environment. They begin to learn from their senses, including smell, sounds, sight, touch, and taste.

Maria Montessori concluded that young children could absorb the most amount of information and develop more rapidly than any other age group—due to her observations of their quick learning process of language and mobility. The brain capacity of young children allows them to function on a basic human level in their first few years of life. During this period of the child's life, Montessori education focuses primarily on coordinated movement, speech, and independence—promoting confidence in the child and the ability to find their place within their society.

Once children are 3 years old, they begin to take on activities to help them achieve coordination and control of movement as they explore their surroundings. In Montessori, tasks are set for the children to help them develop their self-discipline, will, concentration, and self-confidence. These activities are to help the child learn how to take care of themselves and their environment. Specific activities include setting the table, washing up, tidying up after themselves, arranging flowers, etc. These actions will help the children become more civilized as they learn manners and courtesy.

At this age, children are more in tune with their senses than their intellectual abilities. Children learn from their materials according to their size, how they smell and feel, how much they weigh and what they look like, etc. These materials help children refine their senses, allowing them to discover their interests and reactions to certain items, feelings, and surroundings. The child develops a better understanding of the world and how they fit into society.

At around age 3, children begin to use their language skills to their advantage. They begin to discover what they can achieve through communication, and their language slowly starts to become more refined, as they are more aware of the properties that it holds. Reading comes naturally to children, and once they have started learning how to write—children begin to develop their writing skills through hearing and touch senses. Children become interested in art, history, and geography subjects, helping them understand the world of language and creating a feeling of unity with humanity and the world.

Montessori materials provide children with mathematical concepts and set foundations for algebra and geometry. When the children use concrete materials that they can independently use and figure out by themselves, they start to develop a better understanding of mathematics and how it can benefit them in everyday life.

The Second Plane is from age 6 to 12. Children have grown out of their toddler phase by age 6 and become more curious about their surroundings. Six-year-olds are imaginative and can even invent imaginary beings in their heads that they cannot see. They want to be part of a group and to feel involved; they start to ask questions and want answers and reasoning to their discoveries. They begin to understand social behaviors and start to make different relationships with different people, depending on whether their interests align or simply if they enjoy their company. Rules and regulation pique their interest as they want to know what they can and cannot do and what will happen if they break the rules. This stage of life is essential for developing a child's socialization skills as they are fascinated by the people around them—they want to spend time with others and show their own personality to the world. At this age, children have multiple interests and have a desire for productivity and abstract thinking.

The Montessori education curriculum is designed to help children stimulate their curiosity and imagination while allowing them to work collaboratively and develop their relationships with others. The children begin to admire their creative capacities and develop their innovative skills. Children begin to ask, "Why?" and their questions are encouraged. The teacher gives the children opportunities to find the answers to their questions before giving them the answer. Children take on projects in pairs or small groups and are encouraged to work together to help build teamwork and social skills. During this age period, the children are presented with historical and evolutionary knowledge—helping them understand human development. The teachers observe the children, offering them a unique experience that aligns with their wants, needs, and capabilities. The results of observation help the teacher determine which opportunities will help the child maximize their potential.

The Third Plane is from age 12 to 18. By this age, children have reached adolescence and want to do everything for themselves, make their own decisions, and ultimately control their own lives. Adolescents are adjusting to drastic physical and psychological changes, as they seek independence and feel the need to rely on themselves. It is a time for critical thinking and exploring deep moral and social values. During this stage, the adolescent feels the need to concentrate on the social aspect of their life and wants to participate in social gatherings and events. Adolescents start to question the world's ways and want to find a resolution and help solve problems that feel personal to them.

Maria Montessori found through her research that 12-year-olds need specific support at this stage of their lives. Montessori thought that when children enter their adolescent phase of life, they renew their social abilities and become more confident and capable of constructing themselves in adult conversation. They no longer want to be thought of as children, and instead, they want to be treated as equals to their peers. Due to their heightened sensitivity, adolescents become very aware of their social situations. They can easily be offended or hurt—this can cause significant insecurities which can interrupt their social development. Adolescents need to be in a supportive environment, complemented by confidence-building challenges and experiences that help them overcome real-life obstacles.

Due to the rapid changes in their bodies, adolescents tend to feel physically fragile and can have phases of total energy to utter exhaustion. Adolescents feel the need to gain validation from their peers. They do not want to be pushed into adult life by another adult—they would like to prove themselves as adults. They want to be seen and appreciated and build relationships based on their actions and contributions. Adolescents need to have close friends and support from others that may be experiencing the same changes. Through their experiences and challenges, adolescents gain empathy and start to understand and sympathize with others.

Adolescents crave real-life experience and want to know how to look after themselves and their community. Their characteristics and needs have evolved, so their environment requires a change to facilitate this new stage of life. Adolescents need to be provided with opportunities that allow them to prove themselves. In Montessori, adolescents are provided with tasks such as cooking meals, building structures, growing and harvesting food, farm work, or voluntary work. Adolescents gain a deep sense of pride from contributing to the community and working as a team. This stage of their life is a time of deep reflection and self-expression through their art, writing, music, or athletics. They are attracted to literature and reading, understanding science, and how mathematics contributes to their life. Another Montessori program involves adolescents taking care of money—they learn how to produce and sell goods in an experience known as a 'micro-economy.' These experiences help adolescents see the world from an adult perspective and help them understand how the economy works —allowing them to build confidence in themselves and feel rewarded for their hard work. Some other Montessori experiences include:

- Creating and selling crafts
- Interacting with adults
- Cleaning up the community
- Sending mail
- Making bank transactions
- Writing shopping lists
- Creating recipes
- Making weekly schedules
- Camping trips
- Group survival exercises

The Fourth Plane is from age 18 to 24, which is the final stage of Montessori development, where the adolescents progress into young adults with a more mature mentality. During this time, young adults are trying to find their place in the world and have a strong sense of financial independence. They will be questioning how they can contribute to the world or make a difference in society. The young adult will be confident and will want to start applying their knowledge and experience to their interests and further develop their skills and abilities on a deeper level. They may want to travel and explore or share their political views with others. They will begin to determine what career path they are interested in and start developing a plan for their future. By age 24, these young adults should be ready to take on life by themselves.

MONTESSORI NOW

Maria Montessori's ideas were far from popular when she opened her first Montessori school. Today is a different story, as Montessori methods have grown exponentially in popularity over the past decade. Parents are opting for their children to be educated in Montessori schools, with some parents using Montessori methods as a rearing technique in the home.

At first, Montessori education methods made a significant impression in America—but with its popularity came the critiques. Other educators started to examine Montessori's ways of learning. William Heard Kilpatrick, an admired professor at Columbia University's Teachers College, published *The Montessori System Explained*, which criticized Maria's methods and gained the attention of other educators who shared the same opinions. After his campaign, Montessori education started to decline in popularity, and by 1920, there were hardly any Montessori schools left in the US.

In the 1950s, an educator from New York, Dr. Nancy McCormick Rambusch, interested in Montessori methods, met Maria Montessori's son, Mario Montessori—who motivated her to restore his mother's teaching methods in the US. A group of New York parents contacted Dr. Rambusch and expressed their interest in founding a Montessori private school. In 1958, she opened a school in Connecticut. Today, the American Montessori Society is the largest organization in the world dedicated to the Montessori approach, with almost 100 teacher training programs and over 1,300 affiliated schools (Mead, n.d.). Montessori schools still use the same basis of methods, including observing children's educational interests and the encouragement of independent learning.

I have written this book to make it easier for parents and educators to understand each element of the Montessori approach and the benefit of incorporating these methods into a child's life. Over the next chapters, we will cover essential aspects of Montessori. We will include important information about weaning children, how to approach weaning, and how to wean a child successfully onto food using Montessori methods. We will talk about playtime and the five characteristics of play, what a Montessori playroom is, ideas for activities, and how to incorporate Montessori play into your home. We will discuss Montessori toys and learning materials, how they work and how children learn from them while playing. Other relevant Montessori aspects covered in this book include sleep schedules, potty training, discipline, and everything in between.

2

THE MONTESSORI APPROACH TO WEANING

All children are individual and grow at their own pace, so as a parent, it can be difficult to determine when the right time is to start weaning your baby. Whether they are breastfed or formula-fed, at some point, your baby is going to need to start consuming solid food, and they may begin to show you signs that they are ready. Starting the weaning process can be confusing and scary, as there is a lot of conflicting information and advice out there, so it can be hard to decide what is suitable for your baby. Babies will not be able to handle solid food if their bodies have not developed properly yet.

It would be best if you wait until your baby is at least 6 months old before starting the weaning process; this is to ensure that their kidneys and digestive system have had the time to develop enough to cope with solid food. Giving a baby solid food too early can increase the risk of obesity later on in life. Babies can survive off of breast milk or formula milk for the first 6 months of their life. Breast milk is considered the best option as it can be easier for your baby to digest, and it also contains immunity-boosting elements that can help prevent infection. Formula milk also provides babies with the nutrients and energy they require until they are around 6 months old. If you wait until your baby is 6 months old to introduce them to solid food, they may even be ready to start feeding themselves. They are also better at chewing and swallowing by this stage, allowing you to introduce them to finger foods rather than just blended food.

Often, parents can mistake their child's new behaviors for wanting solid food. These actions include chewing their fists, waking up more so than usual, and wanting extra feeds in the night. It can be easy to mistake these behaviors for hunger cravings—however, this is normal, and it does not necessarily mean that they are ready for solid food. It may be a sign that your baby is hungry, and you can solve this by topping up their milk or adding in an extra feed. Not all babies are ready to start the weaning process at 6 months, especially those with dietary issues or those born prematurely. It is always best to consult your doctor and ask for advice if you are unsure when to start weaning your baby.

When children are around 6 months old, they may start to show signs that they are ready for solid food. It is important to observe hand-eye coordination, as your child will need this to look at their food, pick it up, and put it into their mouths. Once your baby can stay sitting up by themselves and hold their head steady, they may be ready to start weaning. If you try your baby with some solid food and they swallow it rather than spit it out, this is another sign that they are ready for solids.

WHAT TO FEED YOUR BABY

When your baby is 6 months old, you should start them off with a small amount of solid food to allow their bodies to get used to it. At first, try feeding your baby one to two spoons of food per day and then increase the amount gradually as your baby's appetite progresses. You can purchase ready-made baby meals from the store; however, it can be much healthier and cheaper to blend fresh food for your baby at home. Baby rice is a popular option to get started, as you can add in formula or breast milk so your baby is used to the taste. It may be easier to start with this option—your baby can get used to the texture before introducing them to the world of flavor. Make sure that you thoroughly cook and blend any food that you give to your child.

Try to avoid feeding your baby too much sweet food, as they may start to crave it or favor it over healthier foods. You should add many flavors and textures to your baby's diet. If you introduce your baby to a wide variety of flavors early on, they are less likely to become fussy eaters and will be more open to trying new foods in the future. Babies do not need salt, sugar, or anything added to their food that is not good for them. Sugar can damage their teeth, and salt is bad for their kidneys.

Once your baby is used to being fed smooth foods, you can start to introduce them to mashed and finger foods, allowing them to start learning how to feed themselves, chew, and swallow properly. Your child may be able to begin feeding themselves using a spoon or their fingers, but make sure to keep an eye on them and do not leave them unattended in case they start to choke on their food. Encourage your child to play with their food, pick it up, and feed themselves as it helps to improve hand-eye coordination. Some parents choose to use baby-led weaning, where they allow the child to feed themselves from the start instead of relying on an adult to spoon-feed them. Baby-led weaning can promote confidence and independence from an early age.

Here is a list of foods that you can introduce into your baby's diet from 6 months old:

Vegetables:

- Peppers
- Peas
- Cauliflower
- Rutabaga
- Spinach
- Broccoli
- Parsnips

- Zucchini
- Asparagus
- Kale
- Carrots
- Avocado
- Butternut squash
- Cabbage
- Green beans

Fruit:

- Strawberries
- Pineapple
- Papaya
- Melon
- Peaches
- Apples
- Raspberries
- Mango
- Nectarines
- Pears
- Bananas
- Blueberries
- Kiwi
- Oranges
- Plums

Starch:

- Millet
- Quinoa
- Toast
- Bread
- Chapati
- Pita bread
- Sweet potato
- Rice
- Baby rice
- Pasta
- Porridge
- Oats
- Oatmeal
- Potato
- Cornmeal
- Maize

Protein:

- Lentils
- Beans
- Tofu
- Chickpeas
- Chicken
- Turkey

- Beef
- Lamb
- Pork

Dairy:

- Full-fat yogurt
- Whole milk (not as a drink but added or mixed in with food)
- Cheese
- Cooked eggs

Always be cautious over foods that can cause allergic reactions. Introduce these foods on different occasions so you can observe and see if your baby has an allergic reaction. If your baby can tolerate these foods, you should add these foods to your baby's diet to minimize the risk of allergy in the future. Here is a list of foods that can cause an allergic reaction:

- Fish
- Shellfish
- Nuts/Peanuts
- Gluten/Wheat/Barley/Rye
- Seeds
- Eggs
- Cow's milk
- Soya

During the first year, babies get most of their nutrients and energy from breast milk or formula milk. Milk feeds should be offered after solids and should be the baby's main drink for the first year of their life. Babies are not ready for cow's milk until they are around 12 months old, but it can be used in cooking and added to their meals. You can offer your baby sterilized water during meals, as this is a great time to get them used to using an open cup or sippy cup and drinking by themselves. Avoid offering your baby any sugary drinks as they can cause tooth decay and be harmful to your baby's health.

When your child is around 7 months old, they should be able to eat without help, as they will start to chew and swallow properly. Your baby will have three meals a day, breakfast, lunch, and dinner, and will be open to a much larger variety of food. It can take a while for your baby to get used to different flavors and textures, and it can be easy only to offer your baby foods that they like. If you persevere and keep offering different foods, they will gradually get used to it. Ensure your child's diet is varied so that they receive enough nutrients and get the energy they need from their food. You can feed your baby extra milk if they are hungry between meals.

By 10 months old, you can start to offer desserts such as fruit or yogurt if they are still hungry after their main meal. Babies are observant and learn from watching others eat, so try to eat together with your baby as much as possible. At this age, your baby should be able to eat lumpier, chunky foods and finger foods. It should be easier for them to pick up smaller pieces of food and eat by themselves. Your baby should be able to drink independently. Keep a sippy cup of water at hand, so they can help themselves when they need a drink.

By 12 months, your child will be able to eat smaller portions of the same meals as you; make sure you chop the food into small pieces. You can now offer your child snacks between their meals, such as fruit, toast, or yogurt. At 12 months old, children no longer need to be fed formula milk, but if you are breastfeeding, you can continue to do so for as long as you like. Your child will now be able to drink whole cow's milk and consume full-fat dairy products. Your child may now be able to drink and use a cup unaided.

THE MONTESSORI APPROACH TO WEANING

The Montessori approach to weaning is based on mutual respect between the baby and parent. You provide the baby with the appropriate food and utensils required for them to feed themselves. When you do this, you provide your baby with the opportunity to learn from their environment and gain pride and satisfaction from their independent achievements.

Babies can survive off of breast milk or formula milk for the first 12 months of their life, so weaning them onto solid food before this time is not essential for survival. Instead, weaning is advised from 6 months old so that your baby can develop the skills they need to feed themselves and to prepare their bodies for much heavier food. You do not have to replace milk with solid food; you can combine the two for the full benefits.

In traditional weaning methods, babies are placed in a high chair and fed at a different time to the rest of the family. When using Montessori methods, the child is seated around the table and can eat with the rest of the family. Allowing the child to eat alongside other family members shows the child respect and makes them feel a part of their group. Instead of purchasing a high chair for your infant, consider investing in a booster seat so that your child can sit at the table with you. Another option is to provide your child with their own table, a child-sized weaning table that allows your child to move around and learn independence. A table like this is also an excellent opportunity for toddlers to learn how to set the table and clear away their dishes.

Montessori weaning includes a mixture of baby-led weaning and spoon-feeding. When introducing your baby to solid food, you could start by placing a bowl of pureed food in front of them and providing them with a spoon. You will also have a spoon at hand, and you can feed the baby and allow them to observe what you are doing and encourage them to practice feeding themselves. You could also fill the spoon and place it down in the bowl, letting your baby pick it up and feed themself. Eventually, your baby will start to want to take over, so you can observe them while they practice. They may prefer to use their hands rather than utensils—a perfect way to refine those hand-eye coordination skills. You can then introduce finger foods and watch as your baby finds satisfaction from new textures and flavors.

Shallow dishes are best for your baby at first, as they will find it much easier to pick up their food, and it will avoid food falling off the plate. You should provide your child with practical utensils that fit in their hands, as a normal-sized utensil would fit into yours. Sometimes gadgets such as suction plates can be handy when trying to avoid mess but will hinder the learning process of being careful with food. Placemats can help your child outline where they are supposed to eat and help with learning how to set the table, as they discover where everything belongs on the table.

Your child will learn how to drink from an early age if you start them off with an open cup. The child will also learn the consequences of what happens when a cup is dropped or spilled. Clear cups are helpful for the child, as they know how much is in the cup and can learn how to steady themselves and avoid spilling their drink. When you first introduce the cup, try holding it in place for the child before allowing them to try it out for themselves. You can then let them practice picking it up and maneuvering it. During this time, expect many spills and refills! Every time your child drinks from their cup, they will learn how to do it better next time. If your child only wants to play, throw it, or put food in the cup, this may be a sign that they are no longer thirsty, and it may be a good idea to take the cup away.

Make sure to always supervise your child when they are eating so that you can ensure that they do not choke or hurt themselves with their utensils. If your child is playing and throwing food, it is usually a sign that they have finished eating. Do not punish your child for playing with their food, as this is part of the learning process and is a perfect opportunity for you to let them know that food stays on the table. Once your child has finished with their food, let them know before you take it away as they may give you an indication that they are still hungry.

If you show your child respect and trust during feeding time, they will show respect for their environment. Practice being patient with your child and always be prepared for mistakes and messes made. Once your child gets used to sitting at the table without throwing food around, you may be able to allow them to eat alone. You may be able to get up and move around so they feel as though they are unattended. It is best not to leave your child unattended. Instead, observe from a short distance and see how they get on when you are not there.

Babies are eager to learn and understand what is going on around them. Communicating with your baby during mealtimes can make them feel included and interested in what you are doing. Talk to your baby throughout each step and tell them what you are doing. For example, tell them it is feeding time and let them know what they are about to eat. Continue to interact with your child as they eat; ask them if they are enjoying their food or want more water. You can use baby signs to communicate and encourage your baby to do the same. Your baby may not respond, but they constantly watch and listen to you and will eventually start to show you signs of what they want. If your baby feels like they can communicate with you, it may prevent tantrums or food throwing as they will be able to tell you if they have finished or if they want something more.

MONTESSORI CHECKLIST

- **Placemats**: A placemat will help your baby learn where to place their plate, cutlery, and drinking cups. Using a placemat is a fun way of letting your child set the table.
- **Mugs, Glasses, and Pitchers**: Allowing your child to use a pitcher to pour their glass of water promotes self-sufficiency, improves fine motor skills, and enables them to access water when they need it. Consider using tempered glass as it is less likely to break.
- **Bibs**: Using a bib that your baby can easily apply and remove allows your child to participate in the process and improves independence. Use soft bibs that are comfortable for your baby to encourage them to wear them.
- **Weaning Chair**: A child-sized table and chair are

considered best when weaning using Montessori methods. Your child will feel valued and feel a sense of belonging when they have a dedicated area that belongs to them. It is a safe way to allow your child to move around freely and prevents them from feeling trapped as they would in a traditional high chair. Your child can also use this table and chair for playing and learning as well as eating. If you want to include your child in family mealtime, you could provide a booster chair and seat your child at the family table.

- **Clear containers**: Use clear containers such as clear boxes, spray bottles, bags, buckets, jars, and watering cans. Using transparent materials will help your child learn independently, as they can see for themselves what is in the container, how much is left, and if it will be of any use to them. It will help them to refine motor skills through pouring and refilling the containers. Your child will not have to ask for help, as they will be able to see for themselves. For example, you can let your child help water your plants. "The transparency also helps the child to make spontaneous scientific connections, such as linking the volume of the water to the weight of the can or observing the movement and flow of liquid as it is poured out onto the plants" (Transparent Watering Can, n.d.).

- **Toddler Kitchen**: Allow your child to have an environment where they can complete tasks independently and help themselves to snacks and refreshments. A toddler kitchen is an excellent way of promoting healthy eating as you can provide your child with healthy snacks that they can choose to prepare for themselves. The kitchen space should be tidy and straightforward to use, with a dedicated place for each item. It should be easy for your child to find items and put them away to help them learn essential life skills and independence. The kitchen should contain a small refrigerator, a water dispenser, a child-sized table and chair, shelves that your child can reach, appropriately sized glasses, bowls and plates, placemats, a bin, and cleaning supplies (such as a water spray bottle and tea towels).

MONTESSORI APPROACH TO PLAY

When Maria Montessori observed the children, she concluded that they preferred reality over pretend play. Once the children got used to the Montessori environment, she introduced traditional toys to see how the children would respond. She realized that the children didn't show as much interest in the conventional toys as they did with practical activities that served a purpose. These practical activities have become an essential aspect of the Montessori classroom.

Children are curious and observant, and they develop their interests from things they can see, hear, and feel. They watch the world around them, and their imagination expands from people, places, and experiences that grab their attention. In traditional methods, children are discouraged from playing with and using items not designed to be used by children. Parents and teachers worry about the safety aspect of allowing children to prepare their food, move around independently, and use materials that could potentially be dangerous. In Montessori, children are encouraged to practice real-life activities while being observed and supervised, ensuring they are safe and secure. At some point, you will have to expose these activities and materials to the children. Children will learn the value of these items and activities early on in life and the consequences of misusing them, for example, dropping a glass or allowing it to spill.

Young children are impressionable and full of imagination. Although most children enjoy fantasies, such as fairy tales, it can be easy for them to mistake fiction for reality. Exposing your child to too much fantasy at an early age can affect how they socialize with others and make it very hard for them to understand the real world. The child may start to imagine these stories happening in real life, which can be scary and can cause nightmares as children do not understand that it is not real. Try explaining the difference between fiction and reality, and tell your child stories about real-life people and places. Instead of only allowing them to read fiction, introduce history books that explain historical events. Tell your children stories about fundamental topics they have shown interest in, such as animals, sea life, science, and geography. Children will find interest in subjects they can be involved with in real life.

THE FIVE CHARACTERISTICS OF PLAY

According to Peter Gray as reported in *Psychology Today*, play generally has five characteristics (Gray, 2008).

1. **Children choose and direct their own play.** In Montessori, children are allowed to play freely and choose what activities they want to partake in. The teacher or parent does not tell the child what to do or when to do it. Instead, they present the children with opportunities and allow them to make their own decisions. In traditional schools, children are allocated activities, usually in groups, which can be entertaining and beneficial for some children, however not for those that do not have any interest in the idea or activity. Allowing the child the freedom to choose gives them the chance to develop in areas more specific to them. Children can follow their natural instincts and have the choice of participating in or quitting an activity. The Montessori teacher or parent will guide the children and provide them with options to make their own choices regarding playtime. The adults will not participate in these activities; instead, they will observe the child and continue providing opportunities relevant to their interests.
2. **The activity of playing is more valuable than the end result.** In Montessori, when a child partakes

in an activity or a challenge, there is no desired result. Achievement comes from the learning process. Children find errors in their ways when they are not getting the results that they want, leading them to repeat their actions and learn from their mistakes. If there is a goal or a means to an end when participating in activities or play, children can become discouraged as they may not find the activity fun or joyful. As children play and discover new activities and toys, they start to set goals and challenges for themselves. Children will feel more satisfied and content when they have completed a challenge they have set for themselves.

3. **Play is unstructured.** Montessori schools do not have specific rules like traditional schools. Instead, there is a structure in place that promotes respect and self-control. A calm environment helps the children to focus and learn. The materials used by the children encourage brain stimulation as focus and effort are required. They begin to learn self-discipline as they come up with ways to structure their play. The children can ask for help if they need it; however, they will not be disturbed by an adult unless it is necessary. The adults will initially show the children the intended purpose of the activity or the materials they are using and then allow the children to proceed by themselves. Children find their interests by watching others, so the

teacher provides examples of how to do an activity or use a material. The children will engage in activities that catch their attention. They will imitate how they have been shown to do something and try their best to achieve the same.

4. **Play is based on imagination.** Children are capable of a lot more than most may think, and they should be presented with opportunities that can prove their abilities. In traditional teaching methods, make-believe and fiction are encouraged to allow children to use their imagination. Children can do this by playing pretend and reading fairy tales. In Montessori, the children have the opportunity to practice real-life events, such as preparing real food using real utensils and reading stories that happened in real life. Instead of filling their minds with false information, the children can grow their knowledge of the actual world while playing and having fun. The world is full of beautiful experiences, people, and places—children do not need to be told fairy tales to be inspired and use their imagination. Children can become more motivated when their fantasies are achievable.

5. **Engaging play means a stress-free mind.** Montessori classrooms consist of a quiet, peaceful, and respectful environment. Children are so engaged in their activities and play that they do not act impulsively or irrationally, as they are too interested in

what they are doing. Children become stressed and
anxious when they feel like they are not in control or
pressured into doing something they do not want to
do. Some people may assume that the calmness and
quietness of a Montessori classroom will mean that the
child will miss out on having fun. However, the
Montessori classroom is quiet and calm because the
children are so fixated and focused on what they are
doing. The children are treated with respect and get to
explore their interests and environments. The children
are so concentrated and engulfed in their tasks and
activities that they do not feel the need to act out or
misbehave.

WHAT IS A MONTESSORI PLAYROOM?

The Montessori environment is an essential aspect of Montessori education, as it is the environment that supports concentration and independence. There are no fancy features or attributes in a Montessori playroom. Instead, the room is simple, clean, and tidy, with a dedicated space for every item and material. The room is spacious and not overcrowded or inundated with toys. All items and materials are displayed to allow children to reach them independently, without help from an adult. Children will learn where each item belongs, picking them up and then putting them back when finished playing. The atmosphere is warm, friendly, and welcoming, and respect

MONTESSORI APPROACH TO PLAY | 49

for the environment is encouraged. There are various engaging activities and toys available to the children.

Having a limited amount of toys and activities will allow the children to maintain their attention, rather than jumping from one to the other. When the children are presented with a wide range of activities and materials, they can find it hard to concentrate on a single action. They lose focus and become distracted by other options available to them. In Montessori, between eight and ten activities are recommended to be exposed to the child at one time. If you have more than ten toys, you can rotate them as your child develops. Switch up the toys and activities according to the child's interests and abilities. If a child is working with one material or activity for a long time, they will eventually absorb all of the information. They will then naturally move on to something more challenging or exciting.

When presenting toys and materials in the playroom, make sure they are visible to the children and stored at the appropriate height. Children will find it harder to choose an activity if it is out of reach; for example, toys put away in a cupboard do not promote engagement as your child has to work to find something before they can start playing. If there is a dedicated space for each material, the child will find it a lot easier to get into a routine of tidying up after themselves. Children will feel a sense of satisfaction and independence from placing their toys back where they belong before moving on to the next activity.

When creating a Montessori playroom, try to keep it clear of obstruction and provide an open space. Children benefit from an open space as they have the freedom to move around and use the area for skill-building activities. It's an excellent opportunity for the children to refine their gross motor skills, as you can create a setup that allows your child to move around, climb, and explore within an open and freeing environment. Having an open space will prevent accidents and allow your child to move around without difficulty.

The Montessori playroom is a neat and tidy environment, where all items are placed strategically. There is a place for each subject or theme, making it easier for children to find everything. It is best not to constantly rearrange the room, as the children will get used to where everything belongs and will be able to pick up where they left off. Demonstrate how to pick items up and put them back, and explain to the children how it would benefit them if they did the same. The children will find satisfaction from placing items back in their dedicated space. Naturally, the children will start to tidy up after themselves without being asked.

There is a difference between toys that entertain and toys that educate. For example, battery-operated toys that light up and make noise will keep your child entertained but will not provide any motivation. Toys that present challenges will help your child to concentrate and develop their motor skills. Allow your child to engage in toys and activities that serve a purpose.

Providing a warm, cozy, and friendly setting in the playroom will allow the child to feel safe and comfortable as they learn. Design the playroom to suit your home, and make the space fun and appealing so that the child enjoys being there.

MONTESSORI AT HOME

Setting up a Montessori environment at home can be difficult, as you may need to make adjustments to every room of the house. Set it up in a way that suits you and your home. Once you have completed the changes, it will become a lot easier to implement Montessori methods in your home. Your whole family can benefit from having a more minimalistic and simple environment.

Starting with the playroom, make sure it is in an open space containing only necessary items that the child will use. If it has no place, store it or give it away. It can be difficult to determine which toys to throw away and which to keep. Consider getting rid of broken or damaged toys and those that have duplicates or serve the same purpose. As mentioned before, electrical toys that light up and make noise are no good for skill-building. Keep toys that are practical and effective. The environment should be peaceful with pleasant surroundings.

If possible, allow your child to decorate their bedroom, guiding them with options that will provide a Montessori environment. Allow them to pick from calm and neutral colors instead of loud, distracting colors. You can also create a calming environment by using essential oils like lavender and tea tree. Ensure all storage, including shelves, drawers, wardrobes, and hooks, are placed at the appropriate height for your child. Your child will be able to access their clothes, toys, and belongings without having to ask for help. Your child will also be able to put items back where they belong. Make sure that decorative items like artwork are visible to the child so that they can appreciate them. Include a laundry basket and a waste bin to promote the upkeep of the bedroom. Save most toys for the playroom, keeping a limited amount of toys and books in the bedroom.

In the bathroom, create convenience for your child. Include a fold-away stool so your child can reach the sink and light switch, etc. Attach a mirror to the wall suitable for your child's height, or have one that is easily accessible. Having access to a mirror will encourage your child to maintain their cleanliness.

In the kitchen, dedicate a low, accessible cupboard for your child. Include plates, cups, and cutlery so your child can prepare their own food and refreshments without having to ask for help.

Find a place in your home that you can dedicate to meditation, thinking, and calming down. This space is not to be intended for discipline, rather the opposite. You can sit here with your child and practice meditation and breathing, art, or exercise. Allow the space to be a place in the home where you and your child can express feelings, think deeply, and meditate.

ACTIVITY IDEAS

In a Montessori classroom, activities are presented to the children so they can choose for themselves. The children have materials like food, drink, and cleaning supplies. They can access and prepare snacks and refreshments, for example, spreading crackers, cutting bananas and apples, squeezing oranges, and pouring water. Tidying and washing up are encouraged, as the children find satisfaction and entertainment from these real-life activities. These projects are available to the child at any time, under supervision, to work with as they see fit. Hygiene is a vital life skill, and children are always encouraged to wash their hands. Soap and water are readily available at all times. Most children are interested in what adults do, from cooking to cleaning; they want to participate and be involved. Cleaning materials like spray water bottles, cloths, mops, and brooms are always at hand. The children can use these supplies to practice cleaning windows, mopping, and dusting—improving confidence and independence while developing life skills.

Most of the activities that are used in Montessori classrooms can be incorporated into the home. Once you have prepared your home for Montessori methods, it should be easy to provide Montessori activities. Start by introducing one activity at a time, and allow your child to process, practice, and exercise before moving on to the next one. Throughout your day, as you complete your own daily tasks, your child needs to be occupied. You can entertain your child by including them in housework activities, such as cooking and cleaning. At breakfast time, allow your child to prepare their food. Give them access to breakfast foods like cereal and milk and allow them to serve themselves. Other foods your child can prepare for themselves safely include bread, yogurt, fruit, and vegetables. At mealtimes, encourage your child to set the table. When it comes to garments, allow your children to dress themselves and only help if necessary. Encourage your child to place their dirty clothes in the laundry basket and demonstrate the steps of doing laundry. Give your child the opportunity to practice using the washing machine and dryer, how much detergent to use, and the effects of mixing clothing. It's unbelievable how much children can enjoy doing these day-to-day activities! Promoting these life skills early on will stop your child from struggling with these activities later on in life. Other activities that you can do at home include stripping and making beds, tidying away toys and clothing, and helping to groom and feed pets.

There are many Montessori activities for children, and they differ depending on the age and level of development. Here is a list of some activities for children from birth to 3 years old, inspired by *The Montessori Notebook* (The Montessori Notebook, 2016c):

Activities for Zero to 6 Months

- **Reading**: You can start reading with your child from birth. Introduce real books that will interest your child. Reading to your child at an early age can help improve language development.
- **Dancing**: Play music, sing, and dance with your child from birth. Listening to music together can help you bond with your baby. Dance with your baby in front of a mirror or while they lay on their mat. Dancing will encourage movement and stretching.
- **Rhyming**: Entertain your baby with rhythmic sounds and poems and allow them to explore different tones and sounds.
- **Self-expression**: Allow your child to express themselves with funny faces, sounds, and expressions. Pay attention to your child while they share these moments with you.
- **Mobile**: A mobile will help your child to focus and improve visual development.
- **Musical box**: A classical musical box will grab your baby's attention and can also help to distract them when you are changing their diaper.
- **Conversation**: Talk to your baby throughout the day. Let them know what you are doing, and listen to them when they try to communicate with you.
- **Paper figures**: Use reflective paper to make figures

that move. Your child will enjoy watching them, which helps to improve visual development.

- **Interlocking Circles**: Place these wooden rings in your baby's hand and let them explore. Your baby will more than likely pull them apart and then try to figure out how to put them back together. It will improve your child's focus and grasping skills.
- **Non-toxic rubber ball with soft spikes**: Your baby will enjoy the feel of it in their hands. It can help a teething baby soothe its gums and can improve grasping skills.
- **Colorful ball**: A colorful ball will help your baby's visual development and grasping skills. Find a three-colored ball, with red, blue, and yellow. Make sure that the ball is the appropriate size for your baby.
- **Bell**: String a ribbon onto a bell and dangle it above your baby. Your baby will enjoy the sound and will reach to grab it. It will help with auditory and visual development and improve grasping skills.
- **Items around the house**: You can entertain your baby with simple things from around the house. Use a spoon, keys, clothes pegs, and bracelets. Manipulating objects will help with grasping skills. Before you give any item to your baby, make sure they don't pose any risk.
- **Rattle**: Give your child a rattle made out of natural materials like bamboo. Your child can shake it and

experience the sounds they make. This will improve grasping and auditory development.
- **Instruments**: Get your baby a set of wooden instruments that they can shake and bang together. Introduce metal to give them a different sound experience. Allowing your baby to hear and explore different sounds will help with auditory development.

Activities for 6 to 18 Months

- **Suction cup toy**: You can use the toy in the bath, in the car, at the dinner table, wherever you stick it down. Your baby will be able to reach for the toy without it moving around. It helps to improve grasping skills and hand-eye coordination.
- **Basket with favorite toys**: Pop two or three of your baby's favorite toys into the basket. Rotate the toys as your baby's interests change. You can allow your child to choose which toys go into the special basket and then which toy they would like to take out. It helps with independence and hand-eye coordination.
- **Soft knit ball**: If you're any good at knitting, knit a ball for your baby. Your baby will enjoy maneuvering it in their hands as they stick their fingers through the holes. This activity helps with gross motor movement.
- **Wooden cylinder with bell**: Show your baby how the bell works, and then place it down near your baby,

slightly out of their reach. Your baby will be
encouraged to move their bodies to reach the bell. It
helps with gross motor movement and auditory
stimulation.

- **Ottoman**: When your baby is starting to pull
themselves up, a heavy-duty, sturdy ottoman will
act as an aid. It should be at your baby's stomach
height. Introducing this kind of object will allow
your baby to pull themselves up and stand
independently. It helps with gross motor
development.

- **Wooden egg and cup**: Your baby can practice
taking the egg out and placing it back into the cup.
Some parents like to use real eggs and allow their child
to take an egg out of the carton and pop it in the cup. It
will help with hand-eye coordination, and your baby
will love it.

- **Wooden cube in a box**: You can hand make a box
to fit around a wooden cube. Allow your baby to
practice putting the cube in and then taking it out. The
tighter the cube goes into the box, the more
challenging it will be for your baby. It will help to
improve hand-eye coordination.

- **A basket full of balls**: Fill a basket with balls of all
different shapes, sizes, and textures. Allowing your
baby to experience different objects will improve their
sensory development. A basket full of balls can provide

tons of fun for your baby while helping to enhance gross motor movement.
- **Stairs**: Once your baby has started walking, they may want to explore the stairs. Allow them to practice climbing up a few steps and then coming back down. Stay close, and do not leave your baby unattended. Stair practice will help with gross motor movement.
- **Wooden rocking rings**: The base rocks so that it won't fall over when your baby attempts to place a ring on the base. It will provide tons of fun and focus for your baby and help with hand-eye coordination.
- **Spinning top**: Try a colorful spinning top and show your baby how it works. Your baby will want to test it out for themselves. It will help to improve gross motor movement, and your baby will love trying to figure out how to spin it.
- **Lock and keys**: Have a look around your house and see what you can find, whether a music box, a padlock, or simply just a key in a door. Always supervise your baby when allowing them to use keys. Show your baby how to lock and unlock the object, and it will allow your baby to try it for themselves. It will help with hand-eye coordination.
- **Cabinets and drawers**: Place your baby's favorite toys or items into a cabinet or drawer. Let your baby explore and find the items. It will help to improve gross motor movement.

- **Art**: Your baby might not be able to draw yet, but if they can hold a crayon, they may be able to scribble on a piece of paper. Provide your baby with different color paper and crayons. You could also use a chalkboard, starting with white chalk and later introducing color. Introduce finger paints, and see what your child enjoys best. It will help your baby to improve fine motor skills and allow them to express themselves.
- **Nuts and bolts**: Under your close supervision, your baby will enjoy working out how to fit them together, helping to improve hand-eye coordination.
- **Table wiping**: Once your child can walk, you can provide them with a cloth and allow them to wipe the table. Your baby won't be able to clean the table at this age properly, but it will introduce them to taking care of their environment.

Activities for 18 Months to 3 Years

- **Matching cards**: You can either purchase or print out your own on laminated paper. Create cards that match up with real objects, for example, a toy car. Let your baby match up the card to the item. Talk to your baby and tell them the name of each object. It will help to improve language development.
- **Taking care of plants**: Provide your child with a watering can and allow them to water the plants. If

your child has a spill, give them a cloth and see if they want to clean it up. It will help your child get used to looking after the environment.
- **Climbing**: Toddlers love to climb, and it is great for developing gross motor movement. Take your child to the park, or set up a climbing frame at home. Stay close and be there to aid your child if they need it.
- **Sliding**: A low slide that your child can climb by themselves will help with gross motor development. If you have a slide in your yard, it is a great way to get your baby moving and out in the fresh air every day.
- **Swinging**: A low swing that your baby can access themselves would be preferable. It will help with gross motor development.
- **Sandpit**: Your child will enjoy the texture of the sand. You can also provide a jug of water so your baby can wet the sand. It will help with motor and sensory development.
- **Hair brushing**: Provide a mirror and a hairbrush and allow your child to brush their hair and decorate it (if they want to). It will help them to learn self-care.
- **Flower arranging**: This is a fun activity that you can do together with your child. It will help them to learn how to take care of the environment.
- **Cleaning shoes**: This activity helps your child to learn self-care.
- **Preparing food**: You can let your child spread butter

on crackers, squeeze orange juice, or cut a banana. Allowing your baby to prepare their food will help with introducing new and healthy foods into their diet.
- **Using scissors**: Provide blunt scissors that are the appropriate size for your child's hands. You could draw a straight line on a piece of paper and allow your child to cut along the line. Closely supervise your child when they are using scissors. It will help the development of tactile senses and vocabulary.

THE MONTESSORI TOY GUIDE

Montessori methods are based on simplicity and allowing children to learn independently. The Montessori environment is uncluttered and seemingly underwhelming—as overwhelming a child can cause distraction and hinder the learning process. Instead of offering a mountain of toys and activity options, a Montessori classroom or playroom is spacious with limited materials. Most objects are made from natural materials like wood. Wooden toys are more durable, better for the environment, and much safer than plastic alternatives.

A Montessori toy should encourage children to engage, focus, and absorb information. Children should be able to hold, touch, feel, taste, smell, and explore each toy so that they can essentially develop their senses while playing and having fun. If the child can manipulate the toy on their own, they will naturally improve their motor skills. Ultimately, a Montessori toy should give children the opportunity to use their imagination and creativity while working with the toy independently.

Throughout this book, I have written about Montessori materials. Now I would like to explain the value and purpose of these materials. Maria Montessori used the term 'materials' over 'toys' because they are intended for much more than entertainment. The items available in Montessori are set out to help the children develop multiple skill sets. There are three main characteristics of Montessori materials:

1. **Sensorial**: A child's sensory development is just as important, if not more important, than their physical development. Studies have proved that sensory learning is the foundation of early brain development. "Starting from birth, children need an abundance of sensory information to build the neurological connections essential to human intelligence" (Age Of Montessori, n.d.). Children, particularly between the ages of 3 and 7, are in the period of sensory formation —meaning that sensory development plays a large part in their intellectual growth. In Montessori, appropriate materials are utilized to promote sensory development. The items are made from natural materials, providing a hands-on, sensory-stimulating experience as the child can feel, see, taste, and explore each object.

Materials vary in size, shape, and color, providing the children with visual and physical judgment and understanding of dimension.

2. **Practical Life**: Children love to get involved with day-to-day activities like cleaning, food preparation, and getting dressed. Learning these life skills from a young age will help develop motor skills and promote independence and confidence. "Through practical life lessons, children develop small and large motor skills, balance, hand-eye coordination, problem-solving, independence, confidence, and more" (Age Of Montessori, n.d.). Montessori classrooms and playrooms include appropriate-sized real-life tools and materials that the children can access at any time.

3. **Academic**: It is sensorial and practical growth that sets up the child's brain for academic learning. In Montessori, educational materials are used to promote engagement and maintain attention. The objects are scientifically designed to allow for error, teaching the children inner discipline as they control their mistakes and improve judgment and comprehension, developing their skill upon each attempt. Children learn the foundations of scientific and mathematical concepts via simple materials like rods, spindle boxes, and beads. Montessori language development materials include phonics cards, moveable alphabets, and letters made of sandpaper.

FIVE CHARACTERISTICS OF MONTESSORI TOYS

The Montessori environment needs to be plain and simple, providing a calming and nurturing space. Select toys that promote learning and stick to natural and sustainable materials like wood. There are five characteristics of a Montessori toy as suggested by Monti Kids (2020):

1. **Montessori toys are simple**. Young children need toys that are simple and easy to use. They need to be able to understand and interact with a toy to learn from it. Toys that provide too much information can confuse a child and distract them from the learning aspect of the toy. Montessori toys are plain, straightforward, and easy for the child to play with while offering key learning elements. A Montessori toy does not include artwork or branding; think basic wooden puzzles and boxes with holes for shape organization. Have toys that stimulate the brain and promote motor skill development.
2. **Montessori toys are based on reality**. Using toys that give irrelevant information like random sounds and visuals will not provide any skill-building opportunities. It may instead distract your child from learning. Present your child with toys that offer actual results and outcomes, and encourage repetition. Toys

that provide room for mistakes and error will help your child focus, repeating their actions until they get the desired results. Montessori toys do not have to be complicated; they are simple with a limited purpose.

3. **Montessori toys are made of natural materials**. Using raw materials like wood and metal is much safer than artificial alternatives like plastic. Although plastic toys can be more affordable, they are easier to break and do not last long. Small children have a habit of putting whatever they find into their mouths, so stay away from materials made from harsh chemicals. Wood and metal are both safe materials and are easy to keep clean. Children are interested in the materials they are using and study their size, weight, taste, and texture. Children gain satisfaction from materials like wood, as all wooden items have a unique texture. Wood and metal come in various shapes and sizes, allowing your child to explore each item from a different perspective.

4. **Montessori materials are functional and constructive**. Toys that do not offer interaction are useless for your child's development. Each toy should serve its own purpose and allow for a particular skill-building exercise. The toys promote engagement and do not work without participation. The children have to explore and interact with the toy to figure out how it works. An adult does not prompt the children to use

the toy in a specific way—the child is left to come to their own conclusions.

5. **Montessori limits play choices**. Try not to have too many toys, as children need to gather information without being distracted by other possibilities. Children need time with each toy to focus and complete the challenges that the toy presents. If there are too many toys available at one time, your child will quickly become distracted and won't stick with one toy long enough to experience the educational benefits. If you have many toys in your house, consider putting some away. Rotate the toys and introduce new ones as your child develops and requires a new and more exciting challenge.

Best Montessori Toys for Babies and Toddlers

Some great toy options for babies include:

- Object Permanence with Tray (available at pinkmontessori.com) is a popular Montessori toy that promotes motor skill development and hand-eye coordination. The objective is for the child to drop the ball into the hole and watch as it rolls back into the tray. The toy helps to improve hand, wrist, and finger control as the child practices precise hand movements. The toy provides the child with satisfaction as they see their actions have been successful.

- The Punch and Drop Toy (available at amazon.com) includes a wooden box, three wooden balls, and a small hammer. The child can use their hands or the provided hammer and whack the balls into the box. The ball will fall into the box and is retrievable from a small hole at the side of the box. The toy helps to improve motor skills, motor responses, and visual perception.
- The Baby Teether Ball (available at greatergood.com) is a teething ball that is one single color, shaped to offer an easy grasp, and squeaks when squeezed. This toy will help your child through the teething process while providing them with the objective of squeaking the ball. You can emphasize the ball's color when giving it to your child, allowing them to recognize and differentiate color.
- The Bell Rattle (available at etsy.com) is a classic Montessori toy with a wooden handle and a bell on either end. This rattle is lightweight and easy for your baby to hold. Babies love exploring sounds, and this rattle is perfect for satisfying your baby's desire to make noise. Your child will determine the origin of the sound, observe the bells, how the bells work, and the action needed to create the sound again. This toy is excellent for infants and can be used from around 2 months old.
- Baby Gym (available at amazon.com) is a baby gym that is simple and doesn't take up too much space in

the home. The gym is excellent for hand-eye coordination development and can support babies starting to stand up and learning to walk. It is small and lightweight, making it easier to travel. The toys that are attached can be removed or changed to suit the baby's level of development.

- The classic 'Skwish' toy (available at amazon.com) is made of wooden dowels and balls held together with rubber elastic. This toy has been designed for small hands to help develop motor skills. Babies can use this toy to grasp, pull, rattle and twist. The material is safe for teething babies and is suitable for babies from 3 months old.

- The Airplane Mobile (available at amazon.com) doesn't take batteries, so it doesn't automatically move or make any noise. Instead, the mobile moves from flowing wind like a draft from the window or opening and closing a door. The mobile is not overcrowded with hanging toys; there are five simple airplanes made from wood material, allowing the child to focus primarily on the shape of an airplane. The toy can be used over a crib or a stroller and is incredibly relaxing for your baby, promoting a calming environment at bedtime.

- Rattling Roller (available at amazon.com) is a toy great for children at around 6 months old or those that are ready to start crawling. The toy is made from wood, containing a wooden ball inside that makes noise as you roll the toy. It is an excellent toy for children learning how to crawl due to its rolling abilities. When the toy rolls away from the child, it encourages them to move and chase after it. The toy also provides satisfaction from the sound of wood-on-wood.

As babies develop into toddlers, they require more brain-stimulating activities. Here are some great toy options for toddlers:

- The Sink and Stove Set (available at amazon.com) includes an actual working faucet and drain, just like the real thing. This set is an excellent addition to any Montessori kitchen; children can practice washing dishes and filling glasses and jugs of water. The set is made from plastic, making it much easier to keep clean. This set is suitable for children aged 3 years and up.
- Play Silk (available at hearthsong.com) is super versatile and offers a wide variety of possibilities. The texture is soft, smooth, and comforting for your toddler. Play silk promotes imaginative play, and children can use the silk for capes, curtains, flags, blankets, forts, or wherever their imagination takes them. They can also be used for arts and crafts and are easy to keep clean.

- The Pint-sized Toddler Table and Chairs Set (available at landofnod.com) is perfect for mealtimes and weaning. With a minimalistic design, there are no distracting features. Children can use the table and chairs for independent play, painting, artwork, or preparing and eating food and snacks.
- The Mirror Blocks Set (available at guidecraft.com) is made up of wooden blocks that are considered the ultimate Montessori toy, as they are made out of natural materials and offer a variety of skill-building opportunities. This particular set features different shapes and mirrors, focusing on science, block play, visual perception, and size proportions. This toy is suitable for ages 2 and up.
- The Schleich Barn Playset with Animals (available at amazon.com) is perfect for animal lovers or introducing children to the animal world. Every piece is precisely detailed and realistic. This lifelike toy has been carefully designed to inspire imaginative play using actual-life objects. It is suitable for ages 3 and up.
- Wooden Stacking Rings (available at lehmans.com) are a Montessori favorite. This toy is made entirely of hardwood. Each ring is a different size and color; the toy's purpose is to stack one ring on top of the other, slotted over the base. It is perfect for refining motor skills and problem-solving and suitable for 18 months and up.

And, finally, here are some toys that grow with your child:

- The Wooden Block Set (available at mother.ly) is the perfect example of a Montessori staple toy. The blocks are simple, natural, and effective. Suitable for all ages, wooden blocks offer endless play and skill-developing opportunities. Children can use their imagination and creativity and incorporate wooden blocks into numerous activities. Wooden blocks present learning opportunities such as balance, sorting, organization, spatial awareness, and coordination.
- Soft Zone Toddler Blocks (available at amazon.com) are large foam blocks that are a perfect staple for a Montessori classroom or playroom, and children of all ages can use and enjoy them. Children can develop movement and motor skills as well as hand-eye coordination. The bright-colored blocks help children identify and separate colors while stimulating dexterity, imagination, and spatial recognition. The blocks are soft and lightweight, so children of all ages can pick them up, build, stack, and play. They are suitable for all ages.
- Ramp Racer (available at amazon.com) is a satisfying toy that is popular among babies, toddlers, and young children. The ramp racer includes four wooden cars and a four-level ramp. Once the car is placed on the top ramp, it races down one level at a time. This toy

teaches cause and effect while improving gross motor skills and hand-eye coordination. This toy is suitable for ages 18 months and up.

- The Nugget Play Couch (available at nuggetcomfort.com) is machine washable and safe for all ages. It promotes imaginative play as it comes in four separate pieces that you can use in different positions. With its lightweight and soft texture, it can be used for naps, as a couch, a castle, or whatever creative ideas your child can think up!
- The Radio Flyer Classic Walker Wagon (available at amazon.com) is a classic wooden toy popular among babies and toddlers. It serves as a walking frame for babies starting to stand up and those learning how to walk. For walking toddlers, it makes a great push toy, toy carrier, or toy box. With safety in mind, the walker features resistance clickers to prevent it from moving too quickly. A walker is a perfect tool for learning balance and confidence and is suitable for ages 1 to 4.
- The six-piece Rainbow Stacker (available at amazon.com) is an exciting but simple toy that stimulates children's creativity, visually and mentally. The different colors help children to identify and differentiate colors. The children can use the pieces together or separately and can get creative and use their imagination while developing fine motor skills. The stacker is suitable for all ages.

MONTESSORI APPROACH TO SLEEPING

Getting your baby into a sleep routine can be challenging. With Montessori methods, children are allowed the freedom to move around within their sleep environment. The children learn to self-soothe and go to sleep independently. Ensuring an environment in which the child does not feel confined will encourage self-discipline and independent control of sleep.

In Montessori, children are helped and motivated to do things by themselves and for themselves. The same rule applies when it comes to their sleep routine. When children are provided with a suitable Montessori sleep environment, they find it easier to identify their sleep patterns. Children begin to develop sleep management techniques and learn self-control. A Montessori bedroom is babyproofed, spacious, and free of obstruction. The room contains a floor bed and low shelving to ensure the children can access their books and toys. A floor bed is favored over a traditional cot as it allows the child to see their surroundings and feel free to move around without limits. The child has the freedom to get into bed whenever they feel tired. If the child wakes up, they have the opportunity to access their toys and books in a safe environment. Calm and relaxing surroundings will soothe your baby. Leaving a dim light on and allowing your baby to read or play quietly will help them fall to sleep naturally.

Children want to know what is happening and like to have a routine. If your child knows when they are due to sleep, they won't be surprised when you put them in their bed. Many babies cry at bedtime or when they wake up in the night, which is entirely normal. It is OK to give them time to cry a little and see if they can get back to sleep. Allowing them to cry will help them to learn self-soothing and will promote independence. You can observe them from a distance or watch and listen to them through a baby monitor and see how they respond to their own emotions and tiredness.

It is important to note that the baby's bedroom must be fully babyproofed before allowing them to sleep in a bed. It is a good idea to babyproof all rooms in your house. Wherever your child has the freedom to move around, you should ensure that it is safe. Later in this chapter, we will discuss Montessori babyproofing methods and how to implement them in your home.

MONTESSORI BEDROOM ESSENTIALS

Floor bed

A floor bed is either a low bed or simply a mattress placed onto the floor. The mattress should be firm for many safety reasons. A soft mattress can include the risk of suffocation, among other dangers. Babies need a firm and flat surface to support the spine and neck and ensure maximum development.

When introducing your baby to a floor bed, it can take them some time to get used to it. Some parents allow their babies to sleep on a floor bed from the newborn stage. However, it is recommended that you keep your baby close to you at the early stages, especially if you are breastfeeding. Consider introducing your baby to a floor bed before they can crawl, as it may make the transition a little easier. The baby will be familiar with sleeping in the bed before they can crawl around and explore. Be patient, as it can take some time, but your baby will eventually get used to their sleep space, and they may even start to ask to go to bed close to bedtime.

When placing a floor bed, ensure that it is secure to the ground and does not easily move around. Either put it in the middle of the room or a corner against two walls. If you place the bed in the corner, make sure that there is no way that the child can push the mattress around. There is a risk of the child getting stuck between the bed and the wall if the mattress is easily moveable. If you are worried about your baby falling off the bed, consider using a larger mattress, placing a rug or cushions next to the bed, or using a bed rail. Ensure there is space along the bed for your baby to get out by themselves.

Low Shelf

Having a low shelf that your child can reach will allow them to access their books and toys without having to ask for help, which means that at any point, they could pick up an item and start learning. When installing the shelf, keep your child's height in mind. The shelf should be safe, sturdy, and secure. One or two shelves will be enough, as you do not want to overcrowd the room. Include toys and books that are safe and appropriate for the children to use by themselves. Ensure that the shelf is properly secured to the wall to avoid it from tipping over and potentially causing harm to the child.

Artwork and decor

Artwork can help create a sense of calm in your child's bedroom and help to improve visual perception and vocabulary. You can decorate the walls with your child's favorite objects or family portraits to help the child feel close to you. Hang decor low to help the child appreciate and enjoy their environment. Ensure all artwork and wall decorations are firmly attached to the wall —even a crawling baby will attempt to pull them off. To be safe, choose frames and decorations that do not have sharp edges or corners.

Pull-up Bar and Mirror

A neat addition to the child's bedroom, the pull-up bar is perfect for babies learning to pull themselves up. The addition of a mirror allows babies to see their movements, improve their perception, and gives them an open perspective of their room. Babies are intrigued by themselves and enjoy looking in the mirror. Ensure to fasten the pull-up bar to the wall securely and at the appropriate height.

Top Tips

You can apply Montessori methods to all rooms that your child spends time in, including their bedroom, nursery, and playroom. A Montessori environment provides your child with the required setting for Montessori learning and development. Remember, all children and families are different, so always find what works best for you, your baby, and your family as a whole. Here are some tips to help your baby sleep better in a Montessori bedroom:

- Consider waiting until your baby has a sleep routine and is used to sleeping through the night before introducing them to a floor bed. Otherwise, you will have the challenge of getting them used to the floor bed at the same time as getting them into a sleep routine. The floor bed may not work for all children, especially those that struggle to sleep through the night.

- If your child frequently wakes up throughout the night or is highly energetic, they may find comfort from nearby books and toys and eventually settle down and go back to sleep. Alternatively, having books and toys nearby could distract the child and stop them from getting the rest that they need. It all depends on your child's personality and temperament. Observe your child's behavior and determine what will work best for them.
- Floor beds do not work for all children. Depending on their age and level of development, your child may not understand communication, so they may not respond to your directions, like asking them to stay in bed or telling them that it is time to go to bed. If you feel that your child is not ready for a floor bed, consider waiting until they are old enough to understand your instructions.
- Getting your baby into a routine and implementing good sleep habits is more important than getting them to sleep on a floor bed. If your baby is struggling to sleep through the night or is not getting enough sleep, it may be a good idea to keep them in a crib until they are a little older. You know your child best, and if you do not think your baby is ready to benefit from a floor bed, consider waiting until they are more developed.
- You may still prefer for your baby to sleep on a floor bed rather than a crib. Stay calm and practice patience

with your child as they get used to their new environment. It can take time, but with consistency, your child will eventually adapt and settle into a healthy sleep routine.

ESTABLISHING A ROUTINE

Bedtime can be stressful, especially if your baby or toddler does not want to go to bed. It would be best to implement a routine as early as possible and stick to it as best you can. The child's nursery or bedroom should be a quiet, calm, and relaxing environment. Children go to sleep much easier when they feel relaxed and settled down. You can practice wind-down time before you put your child to bed. Avoid being silly with your child at bedtime and instead, encourage them to relax. Include your child in their choice of book or pajamas, as they will feel more in control, and they may feel more comfortable about going to bed. If you have older children, your young child may feel better about going to bed at the same time as them.

An example of Montessori bedtime routine could include the following steps:

1. Pick out and put on pajamas.
2. Brush teeth and use the bathroom.
3. Allow your child to pick out one or two books and read.
4. Say goodnight.

5. Consider checking on your child after a few minutes. Let your child know you will check on them, as it will make them feel more comfortable with you leaving the room.

If your baby has a hard time being away from you, try not to give in when they don't want you to leave. It could just make things harder in the long run, and it may take the child longer to get to sleep. Introduce a comfort toy or a heavy blanket to provide comfort for your baby. Create a calming environment in the bedroom or nursery; use relaxing essential oils like lavender. To help your child unwind, practice deep breathing exercises and meditation. Skin-to-skin contact can also help your baby to relax before bed.

All children are different, and the same schedule does not work for every child. You can adjust your child's schedule according to their personal requirements. Below is a table of some recommended sleep estimates from Small World Montessori School (Small World, 2018).

Age	Recommended	May be appropriate	Not recommended
Newborns 0-3 months	14 to 17 hours	11 to 13 hours 18 to 19 hours	Less than 11 hours More than 19 hours
Infants 4-11 months	12 to 15 hours	10 to 11 hours 16 to 18 hours	Less than 10 hours More than 18 hours
Toddlers 1-2 years	11 to 14 hours	9 to 10 hours 15 to 16 hours	Less than 9 hours More than 16 hours
Preschoolers 3-5 years	10 to 13 hours	8 to 9 hours 14 hours	Less than 8 hours More than 14 hours
School-aged children 6-13 years	9 to 11 hours	7 to 8 hours 12 hours	Less than 7 hours More than 12 hours
Teenagers 14-17 years	8 to 10 hours	7 hours 11 hours	Less than 7 hours More than 11 hours
Young adults 18-25 years	7 to 9 hours	6 hours 10 to 11 hours	Less than 6 hours More than 11 hours

TIPS FOR USING A FLOOR BED

As long as your baby's bedroom or nursery is entirely babyproofed, it is possible to start your baby on a floor bed when they are a newborn. However, as noted before, it is much easier for most parents to have their baby in their bedroom with them, especially when breastfeeding. It is recommended that you keep your baby in a bassinet with you in your bedroom until they are around 3 or 4 months old. It may be a good time to transition your baby at this age as they are more alert and aware of their environment.

The mattress should not be soft, no pillow top or memory foam —you want it to be as firm as possible. It should not be deep. Find a mattress that is about six inches deep or less so your baby is as close to the floor as possible. You can use a low bed frame if you do not feel comfortable with a mattress directly on the floor. Whichever option you choose, ensure that the baby is as close to the floor as possible. Don't forget to regularly lift and clean under the mattress to prevent mold from growing.

For children under 12 months, do not use blankets or pillows in their beds. If you feel your baby may be cold, you can put your baby in a sleep sack at bedtime. If you are worried about your baby rolling out of bed, you can get a bumper pillow and put it at the edge of the mattress to stop them from falling. If the bed is low enough, the floor is carpeted, and the space is clear, there are minimal risks of your baby hurting themselves from rolling off the bed. You could also use a toddler rail, but make sure they still have access to get out of bed.

Once your baby is mobile, they will be able to leave their bed and move around their room—babyproofing is essential! If your child is constantly getting out of bed to play, they will likely go back to bed by themselves or fall asleep where they are playing. This should not be an issue as long as your child is getting enough sleep. Make sure to close the door after putting your baby to bed, as they may get up and try to leave the room. Your child may even learn to open the door, so a gate across the door is a good idea for extra security.

If your baby is unsettled, you may want to go in and comfort them. Do whatever works for you! An alternative would be to allow your baby to self-soothe. You want to encourage your child to fall asleep on their own. Once you have put your child to bed, leave the room casually. Do not rush out of the room or linger to say goodbye—don't make the process any longer than it has to be. Calmly leave the room, and shut the door behind you. Your child might get out of bed and then fall asleep on the floor. In this case, it would be best not to wake your child if they seem comfortable. Otherwise, you will risk waking them up, and you will have to get them back to sleep all over again. If your child fusses or cries when you leave the room, leave them alone for 5-10 minutes. This should give your child time to settle down and come to terms with the fact that it is time for sleep. If they are crying or fussing, don't go straight into them as this can lead to bad sleeping habits and separation anxiety at night. Give them a chance to get to sleep by themselves. Most babies will fall asleep after a few minutes. If your baby keeps crying, there may be an issue, so be sure to go in and check on them. Check their diapers and make sure that they are OK. If you go back into the room, repeat the same process (waiting another 5-10 minutes before going back in). If your child continues to cry after this point, it may mean that they are not tired. Consider going in, opening the curtains, and getting them back up for a while. After around 45 minutes, try again and put them back to bed. At this point, they should be much sleepier and ready for bed.

Transition your baby to a floor bed at the earliest age you can. The sooner they get used to it, the better. Create and use a strict schedule for nap time and bedtime so your child can become accustomed to their routine. Eventually, your child will become mentally and physically prepared for sleep. Stick to your baby's sleep schedule as best you can.

BABYPROOFING YOUR HOME

When you consider transitioning your child to a floor bed where they have more freedom, it is really important to ensure the rest of your home environment is safe. Montessori promotes freedom of movement. When using traditional babyproofing methods, you restrict the child from exploring their environment. Instead of locking everything up, find a way of making the environment safe. Take away any dangerous objects out of the child's reach. In Montessori, the children are provided with hazardous equipment such as knives and tools, and they can use them under strict supervision. Making sure the environment is safe is essential when using Montessori methods. Here are some helpful tips for babyproofing a Montessori environment:

- **Corner guards**: When your child has freedom of movement, they will likely bump their heads and bodies on sharp corners around the house. Using corner guards will give you peace of mind when letting your child roam freely. Corner guards are not usually used in Montessori, as children learn the consequences of bumping themselves, and they avoid doing it again. Either way, safety is always what is most important—do what works best for you and your child.

- **Secure furniture to the wall**: Toddlers love to climb, and when they are free to roam, they will more than likely climb on anything and everything. Heavy furniture can be extremely dangerous if not properly secured. Use furniture anchors to secure all drawers, units, and cabinets to the wall.
- **Put away all dangerous items**: For any cabinets and drawers that your child has access to, take away any hazardous items and store them up high or out of the child's reach. Fill all of the lower cabinets and drawers with everyday objects that will not cause harm. Your child will have the freedom to explore their environment. If you have a cabinet or drawer that you need to keep the child away from, use child safety cabinet locks and ensure that it is entirely secure.
- **Stair gates**: Install stair gates at the top and the bottom of the stairs to prevent accidents. Let your child know that once the stair gate is closed, it is off-limits.
- **Cover all power sockets**: Buy good quality power socket protectors and install them everywhere in your house. Children are curious, and if they find a small hole in the wall, they will more than likely try to stick their finger in it. Ensure that the power socket covers go into the wall firmly and are not easy to take out. If

you see your child trying to play with a plug socket, explain the dangers and why it is off-limits.

- **Put away electrical items**: Find a space in your home out of reach of your child to store away any electrical items. To make it easier for you to access your electrical items, store them in a locked box in their usual place.
- **Secure and cover all wires**: It can be very dangerous if your child has access to electrical cables. They could pull the wire out of place or bite and chew on them. Secure all wires and cables to the wall and cover them using electrical cable covers.
- **Lock windows and move furniture**: Keep your child away from the windows. Make sure you lock them. Move any furniture away from the window to prevent your child from climbing up and reaching it. Consider installing roller blinds, as they may stop your child from wanting to explore the windows.
- **Cover the fireplace**: You can buy fire screens, but they are usually lightweight and easily removable. Consider building a sturdy fence around the fireplace to prevent your child from touching the fire.
- **Mount your TV**: Televisions are heavy and pose a risk if they are freestanding. To avoid dangers, you can mount the television to the wall.
- **Stove guard**: Children watch what we do. Your child will watch you cooking, which may entice them

towards the stove. Consider purchasing a stove guard to keep your child away. You could also use knob guards so your child cannot turn on the stove.

As well as babyproofing your home, you can practice safe activities with your child and teach them about the importance of safety. Here are some points to be aware of when practicing safety at home:

- Always supervise your baby when they are in the bath. Do not leave your baby unattended in the tub. Encourage your baby to wash themselves and allow them to move freely, but always under your supervision.
- Wash up together. In Montessori, children are encouraged to wash their cups and plates. If you have a stool for your child, ensure you supervise them on it. Always clean the dishes together as your child may accidentally fall, break the dishes, or put soap in their mouth or eyes.
- Supervise your child on the stairs. Keep the stair gate closed at all times unless you are present. Your child will, at some point, want to venture up and down the stairs. You can let them explore the stairs under careful supervision. If they can access the stairs without an adult, they could fall and seriously injure themselves.
- Keep your child out of the kitchen if there isn't an

adult present. A kitchen contains a lot of dangerous equipment. Montessori encourages children to help out in the kitchen, but this should always be under supervision. You can provide a Montessori child-sized kitchen for your child so they don't have to ask for assistance when they need a drink or a snack. If you cannot lock the kitchen door, consider installing a baby gate.

- Use the appropriate toys for your child's age. You don't always want to supervise your children when they are playing. Otherwise, you would rarely be able to take your eyes off of them. Provide your child with age-appropriate toys that pose no dangers. Ensure that the toys are not small enough to be swallowed. Unless you are supervising, keep all toys that could be dangerous away from your children.

- Always supervise your child when using the "big toilet." Your child can have a potty at hand. Always accompany your child when they go to the bathroom. There have been cases where a child has fallen into the toilet bowl.

- Eat together. When your child is eating, whether at their own table or sitting around the family table with you, make sure you keep a close eye on them when they are eating. Children can easily choke on their food, and they need you to be around to act quickly if this happens.

MONTESSORI APPROACH TO POTTY TRAINING

Starting to use the toilet or potty is a natural process that parents should not force upon their children. Introducing the potty to a child that is not ready can be frustrating and a waste of time. Try not to present negative energy when changing your child's diaper. If your child can see that the smell bothers you, they may start to think negatively about their natural bodily functions. Encourage conversation when changing them, explain to your child what is going on, and tell them what you do when it is your toilet time (tell them that you use the toilet and why). You can place a potty in a dedicated place in your house and explain its purpose to your child without suggesting they use it. The child can then access the potty if they ever feel they want to use it—promoting independence and self-sufficiency. It also gives them time to examine their potty and get used to it being around.

Your child may become interested in the toilet by around 1 year old. Although, they might not necessarily be interested in actually using it. Instead, they may want to flush the toilet or play in the water. You can provide alternative water play by filling a sink or a basin full of water. Once your child is developed enough to dress themselves, you can introduce them to underwear. Even if your child is not potty trained, it's a good idea to let them know what it feels like to be wet and dry. They will begin to learn that being dry is much more comfortable. It may encourage them to hold it in or ask to go on the potty or toilet. You can teach them how to pull their pants up and down using elastic-waisted pants or disposable pull-up diapers. Once they start asking to use the bathroom or go on the potty, you can start toilet training. Teach your child the steps, starting with pulling down their pants and sitting on the potty. Allow them to do this part by themselves and be there to assist if they need it. Explain what toilet paper is and show them how to use it. Once they have finished, allow them to pull up their pants. If you haven't already, this is a great time to teach them hand-washing and hygiene. You should encourage your child to wash their hands every time they have used the potty or toilet.

When your child starts using their potty or going to the toilet, you can set up the environment so that they can continue independently. Keep the potty in the bathroom or a dedicated place in the house so your child can get used to where it is and access it at any time. Ensure that the toilet space includes toilet paper or cloths for cleaning and a laundry basket for wet or soiled clothing. Providing a pile of clean underwear will allow your child to change independently, granting them respect and dignity.

When toilet training a child, make sure to provide the essentials that they need to feel confident when going to the toilet. They may need a stool close by to reach the toilet, so consider keeping one in the bathroom. A parent's role is to encourage the child to use the toilet and not pressure them into it. Forcing a child to use the toilet can discourage a child and negatively affect toilet training.

Consider your approach when asking your child to use the toilet. The way you ask them could impact their response. You want to encourage them, so say, "It's time to use the toilet," rather than asking them, as their answer will usually be no. You can set an alarm clock at regular intervals and remind them that it is time to go. Set a toilet schedule that works for your child's routine. If they are in the middle of an activity, do not disturb them. Wait until they are finished, and then let them know that it is toilet time. Using the toilet is a natural process, and children will learn in time. Be patient and don't punish your child when they don't want to go or have an unsuccessful attempt. The same goes for rewarding your child—don't congratulate them for doing something completely normal.

If your child has an accident in their pants, do not make them feel embarrassed or ashamed. Try not to make a big deal out of it. Don't feel bad or try to comfort them, as it will draw more attention to it. Instead, stay calm and let them know that everything is OK. You can ask them to assist you in cleaning up and allow them to change themselves. Allow them to change at their own pace and stick around in case they need to ask for help. Once they are all cleaned up and changed, ask them to finish up by washing their hands.

PREPARATION—HOW AND WHEN TO START AND WHAT EQUIPMENT YOU'LL NEED

It would be best if you prepared yourself for toilet training when your baby is an infant so you can be ready for what is to come. As mentioned, toilet training is a natural process that should follow your child's pace. Montessori toilet training methods involve respecting the child by including them in all steps of the process.

Consider using cloth diapers from birth, as your child will become aware that they are wet and may feel uncomfortable. Your child will become aware of what happens when they use their diaper. When they have the urge to go, they may start to show signs or let you know. Make sure to change your baby's diaper as soon as they are wet, or your baby may experience discomfort or a rash. Let your child get involved when changing their diaper, talk about what you are doing, and see if they show interest. Consider keeping all changing facilities in the bathroom, and take your baby to the bathroom to be changed.

Your baby will start to understand the purpose of the toilet and the bathroom.

Your baby may start to show interest in using the bathroom or toilet from around 12 months old. It may be before or after, but there are signs you can watch out for to see if your baby is ready. It would be best to wait until your baby is walking to start toilet training so that they can get on and off the potty or toilet by themselves. Your child's body may begin to form a routine, where they have a bowel movement at similar times every day. Another sign that they could be ready for toilet training is when they start to take an interest in cycles. For example, they may observe and follow you as you wash clothing, watching as you go through each step. Babies tend to show interest in activities we do that show results. Don't worry if your baby is not showing any of these signs, as not all babies do. It is recommended that you start toilet training your baby before 18 months old.

Before beginning toilet training, ensure your baby has everything they need to avoid setbacks. Set out a plan and stick to it! Start by purchasing thirty or more pairs of thick, good quality underwear —expect to go through a lot of underwear when toilet training! Ensure the underwear is comfortable and not too tight. This way, your baby can take them off and put them on by themselves. The same applies to pants; always have plenty of clean pairs available as they may also need to be changed every time your baby is wet. Take away any rugs or cushions that your baby could potentially soil. Expect plenty of bedding changes when starting toilet training, as your baby will likely wet the bed at night. Always have clean bedding at hand. Consider purchasing a mattress cover to prevent damage to the mattress. In the car, you could set down a rubber flannel to protect the car seats. It's hard to avoid every accident, so you may have to go through a lot of washing and cleaning. Have stain remover spray and anti-bacterial soap at hand so you can grab and go! Keep the potty in the same place so your child can access it whenever they need to.

Once you have introduced toilet training to your child, you have begun the process. From here, it is important to be consistent and stick with it. Implement toilet training into your child's routine and make them aware of any changes before you make them. Your child observes everything you do, so it is OK to let them see you sitting down on the toilet. Watching you may incite them to imitate what you are doing, and they may want to sit down on their potty. You could take them to the bathroom with you and encourage them to use their potty every time you use the toilet. Your child will start to learn the purpose of sitting on the potty or toilet.

Make sure that you always change your child's diaper as soon as it becomes wet. Your child should be used to the feeling of a dry diaper or dry underwear, and they should feel much more comfortable when they are dry. If they get used to being dry, they will start to hold it in when it is time to go—as they will be aware of the results of soiling themselves. To make it easier for your child when you are home, allow them to move around without pants. It will be easier for them to pull their diaper or underwear down when accessing a potty.

Your child may start to have regular bowel movements at certain times in the day. Observe your child's bowel movements, and make a note of each time they go. You could set reminders for toilet time throughout the day. If you think your child needs to go, calmly direct them towards the toilet and ask them to sit down. Don't worry if it happens before you get to the bathroom—the child will start to recognize the intention behind it. If you do miss the toilet, stay calm and involve your child in the process of cleaning up. If you think a bowel movement is due, but your child is not going, keep their attention by reading a book or talking to them when they're sitting on the potty.

When your child successfully uses the potty, as much as you may want to scream with joy, try not to overreact. Stay calm so your child knows that this is a typical, ordinary task essential to everyday life. Once they have used the potty, physically show them you put the contents into the toilet and flush it down. Explain this process to your child every time you are doing it. Some people like to have more than one potty in different rooms of the house—so the child always has access to one. Wherever you place the potty, keep it there so your child can get used to its whereabouts.

Once you have started potty training, consider getting rid of diapers altogether. Having diapers in the house can make it easy to pop one on for convenience—but it may also set back toilet training. Your child needs to know that you have confidence in them. When leaving the house, you could take a potty with you, especially if your child is not comfortable with using an adult toilet yet. Set the potty down somewhere where your child will feel comfortable, like in a public bathroom or a bathroom at the house you are visiting. Encourage your child to use the toilet before leaving the house, and show them that you will do the same. Explain to your child the benefit of using the toilet before leaving the house, especially if you are going on a long car journey or if you won't have access to a bathroom for a while. Don't worry if they don't manage to go; they will get used to the idea after several attempts. It's a good idea to keep some underwear and cleaning materials in the car in case you need to change on the go!

MONTESSORI-INSPIRED PHRASES

Here are eight Montessori-inspired phrases that you can use to encourage your child through toilet training:

1. "Your diaper is wet. Let's go change your diaper." You can start teaching your child about their bodily functions from the moment they are born. You can do this by simply communicating what you are doing with

them. Let your child know that there is a reason that their diaper is wet and that you are going to help them with a solution (changing their diaper). Your child will start to feel the benefits of a diaper change, as a dry diaper is more comfortable than a wet one. Try not to associate any negativity with changing their diaper, as it may negatively affect how they feel about their normal bodily functions. You want your child to feel comfortable and confident. Including them in the process shows them respect and helps them feel at ease throughout the process.

2. "You're so stable now. Let's try standing up to change your diaper today." Once your child can stand up, you can encourage them to stand while changing their diaper. Allow your child to steady themselves on something for support. You can install a bar in the bathroom or ask them to hold on to the side of the bath or sink—whatever works for you and your home. Now is a great time to move to the bathroom for diaper changes.

3. "Please push your pants down." Once your child is standing, they can start to assist with diaper changing. Provide underwear and pants that are easy to pull up and down. Learning how to get dressed from a young age promotes independence and self-sufficiency. You can also allow your child to assist you in putting their clothes on in the morning and taking them off at night.

This way, they can get used to dressing themselves from an early age.

4. "Would you like to sit on the potty?" Don't force your child to use the potty, as it will only promote negativity towards toilet training. It would be best if you went with the flow of your child. Treat them with respect, and ask them if they would like to use the potty instead of telling them that they have to. Even if your child sits down on the toilet for a second or sits and does nothing, don't stress—it is still progress! Your child learns from every attempt.

5. "It's time to use the toilet." Once your child gets used to the toilet, consider slightly changing your approach. Instead of asking them if they would like to go, let them know that it's time. You are not telling them to go or asking them a question; you are presenting them with the opportunity. If your child is busy with an activity, let them know that they can finish up before going to the toilet. A child will usually say 'no' if asked to do something. Encouraging them to make their own decisions will promote independence. Your child will respond much better to toilet training if they feel like they are in control.

6. "You peed in the toilet just like Mom and Dad." You are not rewarding your child for using the toilet; you are letting them know that they have successfully used the toilet for its intended purpose. Praising a child for

using a toilet is like praising them for sleeping or eating; it's a natural process required as a human being. It can also put pressure on the child the next time they use the toilet, and they may feel upset, or like they are letting you down if they are unsuccessful. Be calm and show confidence in your child. Punishing them for not using the toilet will create negative feelings about toilet training.

7. "You're ready for underwear now." Your child may start to show you signs that they are ready for toilet training. If they are not filling their diaper as often, this could be a sign that they are beginning to gain control over their bowels and bladder movements. Your child may start to ask you about the toilet or tell you that they need a diaper change. Once you have begun the toilet training process, introduce underwear simultaneously—this means completely changing from diapers to underwear. In the first few days, stay at home if you can. Allow your child to access the toilet every 30-45 minutes until a natural schedule starts to form.

8. "Your pants look wet. It's time to change your clothes." Try not to overreact if your child does not make it to the toilet in time. Simply let them know what is going on and offer them a solution. Your child responds to your reactions and feelings, and if they sense negativity, they may feel embarrassed or upset. Ask

your child to assist you in cleaning up. Let them put their underwear in the laundry basket, or ask them if they would like to pick out some clean ones and let them put them on by themselves.

TIPS TO REMEMBER

- Look out for signs of readiness, like if they are dry throughout the day or showing interest in the potty.
- Switch to underwear as soon as you start toilet training.
- Once you start toilet training, be consistent. Try not to go back to diapers or switch from one to the other. Your child may feel like you are not confident in their abilities, and it may negatively affect the way they think about toilet training and wearing underwear.
- At first, if you feel it is necessary, you can use a diaper for your baby at bedtime.
- Remember that if your child has an accident, it is not a big deal. Try to stay calm and confident, and don't get upset with your child.
- Be there for them if they need your help, but allow them to work independently as much as they can.
- Over time, your child will learn that they have to change their clothes when they have an accident. They may realize that changing is time-consuming and

tedious, which may encourage them to hold it in in the future.
- Show them when you put the contents of their potty into the toilet, and then show them what happens when you flush it down.
- Ask your child if they would like to flush the toilet themselves.
- Explain every process to your child as you go along. Show them their routine verbally and physically.
- Let them pull their pants down and pull them back up during toilet training.
- Encourage your child to wash their hands every time they use the toilet.

MONTESSORI APPROACH TO DISCIPLINE

Many people assume that Montessori taught children are allowed to do whatever they want, without punishment. To some extent, this is true—children are given the freedom to make their own choices and explore their environment independently. There are no punishments; however, that doesn't mean that there are no rules. Discipline is approached as a learning opportunity. Others assume that Montessori children are missing out on being children—which is simply not the case. The children are treated with respect, and nothing is forced upon them. They are presented with opportunities and are allowed to make their own choices within a safe and controlled environment. Here are some tips for the Montessori approach to discipline:

- **Offer help when required:** If your child needs your help, they will more than likely ask for it. If your child is upset or frustrated, you will be able to tell if they need your help or support. It can be difficult to communicate with a child that is extremely upset or is having a tantrum. It would be best to help your child calm down before you try to understand the problem. Be patient with your child while they calm down. Once they have settled, you can get to the root of the problem and figure it out together. Your child needs to know that you acknowledge their feelings. When they are having a difficult time, show them that you understand and try not to diminish their feelings. Listen to what they have to say and try to calm them down by encouraging conversation. Allowing a child to express their emotions and feel understood will make them feel safe and comfortable with you. They will know that you support them and that you will be there for them. They will not feel afraid to share their feelings with you—which will allow you to connect with your child on a deeper level. Your child will learn how to control their emotions at a young age.
- **Promote freedom within a limited environment:** Allowing a child to have freedom within a safe and secure environment will give them the opportunity to build their independence while

developing essential skills. If a child has too many restrictions or boundaries, they may start to feel trapped and very limited on what they are allowed to do. The child may feel scared to participate in activities, which could hinder their development. They could also start to do things in secret out of fear of getting caught. On the other hand, if a child has no boundaries or rules in place, they will think that it is OK to do whatever they want, whenever they want, without thinking of how it could affect others. A child with no boundaries may find it hard to feel satisfaction or reward. Find a balance that suits you and your child. Set clear limits and boundaries, and be sure to stick to them. Being consistent with the rules you set will help your children get used to them, and they will become a part of their everyday routine. It will also help you to build a trusting relationship with your child, as you both know where you stand with one another. You can gently remind your child of the rules regularly. You can set up a Montessori home environment that favors your set rules as well as your child's wants and needs.

- **Encourage responsibility:** Children will fall out with each other from time to time, and when this happens, it is a perfect opportunity for us to teach them how to deal with it. Showing your child how you tend to someone that is hurt or upset will encourage

them to do the same. Your behavior towards others
will affect how your child treats people. Show them the
importance of kindness and explain how their actions
can affect others. Children will learn to take
responsibility for their actions. Teaching responsibility
to your child from a young age is very important.
Being responsible will help your child to become
resilient and will give them a sense of purpose.
Encouraging your child to tidy up after themselves,
water plants, or take care of a family pet will help your
child learn how to take responsibility for their
community. Teach your child to look after their
belongings. Don't replace broken items constantly.
Instead, teach your child that if they break something,
it is gone. You can then wait a while to get a new one.
It will teach your child to take care of their stuff. Teach
your child self-care. Allowing your child to dress
themselves, brush their hair, or wipe their nose will
help teach your child how to take responsibility for
themselves.

- **Gentle direction instead of rewards and punishments:** Bribing, rewarding, or punishing a child is like comparing them to another person's standards. Your expectations are coercing your child's actions and thoughts. Children have the capability of developing inner discipline. Providing them with a developmental environment will allow them to detect their errors and mistakes. It will enable the children to make instinct-based decisions and naturally determine right from wrong. Instead of offering rewards, you can allow your child to feel inner satisfaction from their successes. Expecting a reward for every win will be your child's only motivation, and they will feel highly disappointed if they don't get one. Rather than punishing your child when they do something wrong, offer them gentle direction. Talk to your child, and work things out together. Explain the situation and help your child to understand why they should avoid doing it again. Let them make their own decisions, but make sure you give them the knowledge they need to make sound judgments.

- **Talk to each other with respect:** Children learn from us and tend to mimic the way we do things. How we communicate with our children will affect how they communicate with others. We mustn't treat children as though they are inferior to us. They need to know that we value them as human beings and that their thoughts and feelings matter. We must build trust between ourselves and our children as they look to us for guidance and support. Always talk to your child and others with respect. Display manners and courtesy and encourage your child to do the same. Remember that everyone is different, including your child. Get involved with your child's interest and encourage them to engage in yours. Sharing your interests with your child will help them respect other people's interests aside from their own.

- **Help your child to communicate:** You know your child best, so you can help others understand a situation from your child's perspective. Observing your child will help you to translate their wants and needs to others. Show your child that you are there to support them when they need it. If you explain to your child what they are doing or feeling, your child will better understand their actions and emotions. Your child will start to come up with solutions independently. You can also talk about what you are doing, explain your actions and how you feel. If you take responsibility for your own actions, your child will follow suit.

- **Set limits and encourage kindness**: When you set your house rules, make it clear to your children what they are. Be consistent, stick to your rules, and lead by example. Your children will be well aware of the boundaries set at home. From time to time, children will act out, and it is our job as parents to step in and guide them. For example, if you see your child hit another child, you could say something like, "I can see you want to hit, and I cannot let you hit someone. How about we use our words instead?" Explain to your child the consequences of their actions (hurting another). Offer them the opportunity to make amends.

- **Work together, not against each other:** Instead of bribing or punishing your child when they don't want to do something you've asked—work with them. For example, if your child gets frustrated because you've asked them to stop doing something, offer them an appealing and exciting alternative. Present them with options rather than ultimatums or bribes. Show them that they are an essential part of the family by including them in your day-to-day activities. If you reward your child for listening to you, they may start to expect rewards for everything you ask them to do. Teach your child that respect and kindness are an essential part of life.

- **The adult's role:** It is up to us to teach our children the value of kindness and respect. It can be challenging to discipline your child using Montessori methods, as it requires much patience. For our children to take rules seriously, we must follow them ourselves and lead by example. As parents, we are role models to our children. We need to practice what we preach when it comes to rules and boundaries. Take time to learn patience, practice meditation, and instill calmness into your life.

SETTING LIMITS

Montessori methods encourage the freedom of children within a respectful and supportive environment. The approach allows children to make their own decisions instinctively—within set boundaries that are adhered to by the household. Here are some tips to help when setting limits:

Set Clear Boundaries

You do not have to have many rules for the Montessori method to work in your household. You should have a simple set of rules. Be consistent and make the rules very clear to your children. Here are some examples of Montessori house rules:

- We use words instead of physical action to solve disagreements.
- We speak kindly to each other.
- We enjoy our meals together as a family.

Limits With Love

Don't enforce the rules; encourage them. From time to time, children will need reminding of the household rules. Be firm with your children in a calm and loving voice. Be sure to control your anger before approaching your child. Use breathing techniques and calm yourself down. When being firm, kneel down to your child's height and talk to them respectfully. When your child gets upset, be compassionate and understanding and allow them to express their emotions.

Give Reasons

When setting your household rules, think of why and explain the reasons to your child. Your child will want to understand why they are not allowed to do something. If you do not explain, they may continue to ask or decide to find out for themselves. It is always good for children to understand boundaries and consequences. Giving your children the answers to their questions will improve their judgment.

Rules to Suit Age and Abilities

Your house rules will vary if you have children of different ages or as they grow and get older. Set rules that are appropriate to your child's age and capabilities. As your child gets older, they learn responsibility and respect. They may disagree with the rules, and they may become very vocal about it. Listen to your child and their reasoning and carefully consider how they feel. Find a mutual ground that suits you both.

Working Together

You can reassure your child that you want what they want and that you would like nothing more than to provide that for them. You do not have to be in disagreement with your child all of the time. Work together to find alternatives and meet each other's needs.

Be Safe

When it comes to safety and dangerous situations, you have to be firm! You have to make the rules very, very clear to your child. If your child puts themselves in danger, it is essential to act quickly and physically but gently move them out of harm's way.

TIPS FOR MONTESSORI DISCIPLINE

1. Instead of telling your child what to do, allow them to make their own decisions. When you present your child with choices, you are allowing them to discover themselves and their interests. Forcing your child to do something they do not want to do may make your child feel resentful towards you.
2. Try not to diminish your child's wants and needs. If your child has a problem—work together and help them to solve it. Ask your child what you can do to help. If you cannot solve the problem, offer alternatives or encourage communication. Let your child know that you are there to support them.
3. If you give your child too much praise, they may struggle to understand their true abilities. They may feel a sense of entitlement and may expect rewards for everything they do. It may affect how your child treats others, as they may feel as though they are more

superior. If your child has worked hard at a task, you can express your recognition of their hard work.

4. Let your child express all of their feelings. When they are upset or angry, tell them that these feelings are normal and that you also feel this way sometimes. Offer them support and understand things from their perspective.

5. Try not to take sides or get involved with arguments between siblings. Describe their behavior from your perspective and tell them that you are confident they can work it out between themselves.

6. Don't step in unless you need to. Provide your child with the appropriate equipment and environment to work independently. If your child asks for help with something that they can do for themselves, guide them through the process and only help when necessary.

7. Instead of answering all of your child's questions—give them the chance to see for themselves. When possible, physically show your child the information they need to work out the answer to their question.

8. When making decisions that will affect the whole household, make sure you take everyone's needs and feelings into account. It is a good idea to hold family meetings and discuss changes to ensure everyone is happy.

9. Allow your child to explain their actions when they have misbehaved. Don't jump to conclusions and

punish your child. Give yourself time to evaluate the situation and listen to your child. Remind your child of the importance of kindness and respect.
10. Don't label your child. They may feel like they have to live up to this expectation. Praise them for their manners and respect.

MONTESSORI COMMUNICATION TIPS

Here are some helpful tips on how to communicate with your child in a positive way:

Don't Say	Do Say	Why?
"It's not a car. It's a tractor."	"I see a tractor. Did you want to show me the tractor?"	Instead of correcting your child, you want to help them to learn.
"The grass is green because…."	"I don't know. Would you like to find out together?"	Let them find the answers to their questions. It will encourage their curiosity.
"Good job! Well done!"	"I see you worked very hard on your painting. You made good use of the colors."	Give your child feedback on their work, and tell them how it makes you feel. They get satisfaction from their work instead of praise from you.
"OK, it's their turn now."	"They are still playing with it, but they should be finished up soon."	Allow your child to finish playing with the toy. If they are forced to share, they might want to hold onto the toy even longer.
"It's only a sweater. You can wear this one."	"I see that you are upset because your favorite sweater is in the laundry. What do you think of this one?"	Don't diminish your child's feelings. If they are upset, let them be upset. It's better to let it all out.
"Stop fighting!"	"I am here to keep you safe. I cannot let you hurt one another. How about we use our words instead?"	No fighting can be one of your strict house rules. Remind your child of the rules when they break them.
"Don't worry. It's only a little scrape."	"That must have hurt. How do you feel?"	Acknowledge your child's feelings and let them know that you care.
"You shouldn't have done that."	"It looks like you…." "Are you feeling…?"	Instead of blaming them, try to understand the situation and how your child feels.
"You're always spilling things."	"It looks like you had an accident. Do you need my help?"	Don't judge your child—help them to understand.
"Don't drop it!"	"If you hold it with two hands, it will make it easier for you to carry."	Direct them towards success—let them be independent.
"Let's go and do some baking."	"I am going to go and bake. Would you like to help?"	Let your child make their own choice. If they are interested, they will let you know.
"I will do that for you."	"Would you like me to help you do that?"	Give them the chance to help themselves and only step in when you need to.
"You are very naughty."	"I can see that you have been having a hard time. Do you want to talk about it?"	Avoid using labels for your child, as they can negatively impact how children feel about themselves.
"You are the oldest, and you should know better."	"Can you both look after each other while I go into the kitchen?"	Don't expect more from older siblings. Give all siblings responsibility.

STAYING CALM

As parents, it is easy to get stressed out, and it can be a challenge to stay calm. When we raise and teach our children using Montessori methods, we need to be patient and gentle. It is essential for us as parents and teachers to work on ourselves, practice patience, and learn calming techniques. When we get mad at our children or tell them off, it usually worsens things ten times over. Everybody gets worked up, and a minor issue can explode into a full-scale temper tantrum—on both sides. In order for us to teach our children calmness and respect, we must practice it ourselves. Let's talk about some helpful ways you can practice staying calm.

Start the Day as You Mean It to Go On

To get ahead of the day, wake up an hour before the rest of the household. You can attend to your own needs and prepare for the day without any interruptions. Try meditating for a few minutes each morning, concentrate on breathing, and clear your mind for the day ahead. Meditation is an excellent way of gaining control over your emotions; you can think more rationally, become less reactive, and feel less tense. The best thing about meditation and practicing breathing exercises is that you can do them anywhere, anytime. Suppose you find yourself in an unpleasant situation where you feel anxious or stressed—take a moment to think it out and breathe. If your children disturb you while meditating, you can ask them to either join you or allow you some time to finish your meditation. Another great tip for the morning is journaling. Write down all your thoughts, feelings, and your expectations of the day. You can pre-plan activities and make to-do lists. When you plan out your schedule, it makes it easier to stick to a routine and will free up precious time in the long run.

Change Your Mindset

When your child acts out and doesn't listen, it can make you feel like they are against you. Instead of constantly feeling attacked by your children, take a moment to get to the root of the problem. Remember, your children need you for guidance, so when they are upset, they need your support. Listen to your child, and offer them advice and options. Ask them if they need your help, and then solve the problem together. Approaching your upset child with a clear and calm mindset will help them to calm down. You will resolve the issue much quicker. Practice talking to your child in a soothing voice. When you speak to your upset child, you want to show them empathy and let them know that they can rely on you for support. It is the adult's job to make the child feel safe. Let your child express all of their feelings—even sadness and anger. Give them time to let it all out. Try your best to be as understanding as possible. Put yourself in your child's shoes and think about how they may feel. Let your child know that everything is OK and that it is entirely natural to feel these emotions.

Prepare Yourself for Calm

When you set a schedule, you know what's coming. Therefore you can prepare yourself for events that may be stressful. Organize trips to the supermarket earlier in the day to have more energy for the exhausting task. If you take your child out to a restaurant or a place where they will need to sit still, bring toys or books to help keep your child entertained. Fit outdoor time into your schedule every day, even when it is raining. Spending time outdoors can help everybody feel calm. Try not to squeeze too much into one day. Leave some free time in your day and allow your child to play while you reflect, catch up, or take a moment to yourself. In the evening, you can analyze your day and figure out how to make improvements for tomorrow.

Be Aware of Your Limits

We try our best to stay calm, even when our children are doing things that make us feel super uncomfortable. Allowing your child to push the boundaries over and over again will eventually become too much. It can lead you to lose your temper altogether. If your child is doing something you know you are not OK with, approach the situation before it blows out of proportion. If you feel yourself getting worked up or stressed, take a moment to calm yourself and gently address the issue with your child.

Don't Step in if You Don't Need To

Instead of stepping in to help your child resolve their problem, observe and wait it out. Give your child a chance to come up with a solution. Carefully watch how your children respond to challenges. Even if they seem upset or angry, allow them time to calm themselves down. If they are struggling to resolve their issue, or if they ask you to help them, then you can step in and offer solutions. If your children are fighting with one another, give them a chance to work it out themselves. If they cannot work it out, observe and verbally tell them what you see is happening. Even if you feel like one child is in the wrong and one child is in the right, try not to take sides as it could make the situation a whole lot worse. Act as a mediator and explain to each child how the other may be feeling. It will help your children to learn how to resolve disputes between themselves.

Find Alternatives to Punishments and Rewards

Instead of rewarding and punishing your child, work with them. For example, explain the benefits of the task at hand and explain the consequences of misbehaving. You don't have to punish your child; you can help them understand why they can and can't do certain things. Your child will learn how to control their behavior better when they know right from wrong. Try not to judge or embarrass your child when they get something wrong. You can encourage them to engage in activities with you, not for reward, but because it is exciting and fun. When they want to do something you disagree with, offer your child a more appropriate alternative.

Enjoy the Little Things in Life

With busy schedules, busy lives, and children running awry—it can be easy to forget about the beauty of life. Sometimes we can forget about all of the wonderful things going on around us. Remember to take time to yourself—stop and appreciate the small things in life. When things seem to be going wrong, remind yourself of all the things that are going right. Be present and live in the moment. Find your calm and remember how lucky you are to have these tiny humans around you.

Find Solutions That Suit Everybody

For us to be able to take care of our children, we must take care of ourselves. For us to implement Montessori methods, we need to be calm and patient with our children. We cannot do this if we don't give ourselves a break. To keep the peace at home, we want to make sure we meet everybody's needs in the household. Be gentle with yourself and your partner, and acknowledge each other's needs. Prioritize taking time out every once in a while so that you can relax, recuperate, and reflect. Sometimes, a nice, long, relaxing soak in the bath is all we need. Make time for hobbies, reading, and exercise—remember to look after yourself. Find something that you enjoy, and find time in your schedule to make sure it happens.

Create an Advantageous Environment

It can be hard to get things done when our children are constantly asking us for help. We can set up the environment to allow the children to help themselves. When your child asks for assistance, you can make a note of it and figure out how your child could do this for themselves in the future. Adjust the environment to suit your child's requests. Place all items at your child's height so that they have access to anything they need. You can provide them with materials that they can use to clean up spills or messes. Try to make sure they have everything that they need before you leave them to play. When your child wants to do a messy activity, such as painting, make sure you have the time to clean up afterward. If not, find an alternative or only give them a small amount of paint. This way, there shouldn't be much mess, and it won't take long for you to clean up. Your child may even be able to clean up the mess themselves.

Listen to People That Inspire You

Sometimes, it can be hard to resonate with other parents that do not use Montessori methods. They may feel differently about how to raise and teach a child. Spend time with other Montessori parents, talk to your child's teacher, or join online Montessori groups. You can bounce your ideas off of one another, ask for advice, and share tips and tricks. Sometimes, just having a chat with someone that understands can help us feel relaxed.

Connect With Your Child

Spend time with your child and focus on building your relationship. Your child needs to know just how loved they are. When they feel loved, they know that when you ask them to do something or stop doing something, it is because you love them. They know that you are trying to keep them safe, not trying to spoil their fun.

If It Gets to Be Too Much

Sometimes, even when we try our best to stay calm, our emotions can get the better of us. It is normal, and it happens. We just have to know how to deal with it when it does. When you feel like everything is getting too much, rely on your partner. Ask them to take over while you take a moment to calm down and reflect. Do some deep breathing exercises, as it will calm you down and help you think more clearly. Don't be hard on yourself. If you are alone, make sure your child is safe, and go into another room to calm down. Make yourself a coffee or splash your face with water, whatever works for you. Remember, your child is not against you—they are just having a difficult time right now. Once you have calmed down, you can approach your child with a much clearer mindset. By showing your child how you calm yourself down, you are demonstrating emotional control.

End Your Day the Way You Started It

At night, once the children are in bed, it is time to relax and reflect. Take a little time to get organized for the next day so that you can save time in the morning. Think about your day and how everything went, and think of ways you can have a better tomorrow. Find ways to relax and unwind. Take a bath, snuggle with your partner, or watch a favorite movie on TV—whatever works for you. Evenings are the perfect time to destress and put your feet up!

8

KEY BENEFITS OF IMPLEMENTING THE MONTESSORI METHODS

Children raised and taught in a Montessori environment are capable of developing many skill sets. Montessori methods encourage positive characteristics and qualities in children, such as independence, empathy, self-confidence, and self-sufficiency. "Given the freedom and support to question, to probe deeply, and to make connections, Montessori students become confident, enthusiastic, self-directed learners. They can think critically, work collaboratively, and act boldly—a skill set for the 21st century" (American Montessori Society, n.d.).

As we have previously discussed, a Montessori environment is tailored to suit each child's wants, needs, and level of development. In a Montessori classroom, children are treated as individuals, and the teachers observe and present them with opportunities to learn. Every Montessori classroom is designed to help children learn and study independently. All materials and activities are optional, and children can participate at their own free will. A Montessori environment is suitable from birth to adolescence. The classroom consists of children of mixed ages, with typically three years between the youngest and oldest. The different age groups allow for a family setup in the classroom, where younger children look to the older children for guidance. Older children enjoy being role models and mentors for younger children—teaching them independence and confidence.

Children are allowed the freedom to make their own decisions within an environment that has limits. The children learn at their own pace and choose their activities within a community that encourages respect and kindness. The children can explore, discover answers, and come up with solutions to their problems. "Internal satisfaction drives the child's curiosity and interest and results in joyous learning that is sustainable over a lifetime" (American Montessori Society, n.d.). The materials and environment allow for the children to find and explore errors and mistakes. The children learn to repeat their actions—improving their attempts and finding solutions until they are successful. Solving problems helps the children realize their capabilities, improving independence, courage, and confidence. Montessori techniques have proved to develop children's social skills, manners, and emotional control.

FIVE REASONS TO CHOOSE MONTESSORI

There are many ways you could choose to educate your child, so why choose Montessori? There are many benefits of Montessori education, and Montessori methods have been used worldwide for decades. Here are some reasons why you should choose to educate your child using Montessori techniques:

1. **Children are prepared for the real world:** Unlike most traditional schools, Montessori does not base its education on skill-building alone. Montessori methods can help to prepare a child for all aspects of their life. Children are encouraged to practice real-life activities and learn how to take care of themselves and their environment. The children are shown respect and learn how to respect others. When a child is raised using Montessori methods, they gain practical skills that they will use at some point in their life. From being part of the Montessori community, children gain the required skills to become outstanding members of society.

2. **Children are observed and given opportunities that suit their level of development:** Just because a group of children is the same age does not mean that they are at the same level of development. In traditional schools, children are taught using the same curriculum. They are expected

to learn at the same pace as one another and receive similar results. It simply does not work, as every child is different, and every child has individual requirements for their development. If you teach a group of children at the same level, those that fall behind find it hard to keep up. Those that are ahead can find it hard to pay attention when they are not learning anything new. Either way, it can affect a child's confidence. Montessori environments allow for a child to progress depending on their current level of development. Children can work alongside one another, at their own pace, with their own choice of study. The children are all individually observed. From these observations, the children are presented with the environment and materials suitable for their stage of development.

3. **Limited rewards help children learn self-discipline and self-satisfaction:** Children do not benefit from being praised for everything they do. A child that receives rewards for every accomplishment will find it hard to accept critique. In Montessori, there are no rewards. Everything a child learns is left for them to appreciate. Children feel a sense of self-satisfaction when they complete a task and learn to recognize their hard work. Rather than expecting a reward, children find personal joy from their successes. They see how their skills contribute to making life

easier and more understandable. They realize that they are bettering themselves as people. When you praise a child in Montessori, it is specific to what they are doing. For example, you could say, "I like how much detail you included in your artwork." You are not offering rewards or compliments for their work; instead, you show admiration for their determination.

4. **Montessori helps children figure out who they are:** Children can recognize their abilities when they experience trial and error. Allowing a child to come up with their own solutions, instead of helping them solve their problems, can develop their sense of independence. They feel confident when they figure things out for themselves. A Montessori environment provides materials that allow children to see the error of their ways visually. They have the freedom to choose their materials and activities, which means they can make choices based on instinct. In Montessori, children can learn naturally and explore their interests, figuring out what they like and dislike.

5. **Children develop good social skills:** In Montessori, manners and etiquette are just as important as any other skills. As there are only a limited amount of materials in Montessori, the children have to share. They are allowed to play with their material until they have finished with it. They are then encouraged to pass it onto the next child who is

waiting for their turn. It helps teach the children to be respectful to one another and to have patience. Children learn from each other and their environment. When the adults consistently demonstrate manners to the children, they begin to understand the importance of politeness and respect.

FIVE REASONS WHY MONTESSORI METHODS WORK

As noted by a blog post on *Montessori Rocks* (2017), the five key reasons that Montessori methods work are:

1. **Children enjoy learning**: In traditional schools, children don't have much choice; they are assigned work and expected to do it. When you tell a young child to do something, it's like their instincts tell them to do the opposite. In Montessori, the children have the freedom to choose. They can follow their natural instincts and engage in activities of their own free will. When a child decides to partake in an activity, it is because it has piqued their interest. The best thing about Montessori is that the children have fun and enjoy themselves while learning essential skills.

2. **Montessori promotes independence**: Montessori environments are designed to suit a child's size. The children benefit from child-sized tables and

chairs. They have access to eye-level shelves that hold skill-developing materials. The children can use real-life items that accommodate their height and size. They can partake in real-life activities such as cleaning, food preparation, and caring for plants, among many others. Their environment presents all items that a child would usually ask for, allowing them to engage with and complete tasks independently. Children feel a sense of satisfaction and pride when they do not have to ask for help and manage to find solutions by themselves. The materials show the children the error of their ways and allow for independent rectification. Adults can help the children if and when required. The children learn their capabilities when they complete tasks and activities independently. When a child is aware of their abilities, they will feel much more confident approaching challenges in the future.

3. **Montessori is consistent**: Montessori methods are popular worldwide and have been successfully used as a form of education for over a century. Montessori has stayed the same as the methods work, and there has never been a reason to change. The practices have proved to be successful and can be used on a child from birth to adolescence. The Montessori approach is used on each child depending on their level of development. The methods always stay the same but are presented to suit a child's current needs.

4. **Each child is approached as an individual**: In Montessori, all children are observed and dealt with individually. Children are not forced to do anything that they don't want to do. They are gently guided towards activities and materials that interest them. They are always presented with opportunities that are appropriate to their level of development. The aim is to give each child the chance to reach their full potential in all aspects of life.

5. **Children find it easier to understand**: When a child is filled with information without reason or explanation, they find it very hard to understand and remember—because they have not associated this information with any visual or mental interpretation. Children find it hard to absorb information that they do not understand. In Montessori, the children can use materials and activities in various subjects to help them understand cause and effect. When a child finds the answers to their questions, they start to link information together and set foundations for further development.

BENEFITS OF A MONTESSORI PRESCHOOL

Montessori preschools focus on the development of language and muscle movement. The aim is to help children through essential early life milestones. Older preschool children learn from group experiences and participate in group activities such as trips and special events. Younger preschoolers engage in everyday activities such as cleaning, food preparation, arts, and crafts—focusing on improving fine motor skills. The children have the freedom to choose their activities and methods of play. The children are encouraged to play alongside one another, showing respect for each other and the environment. They naturally begin to develop relationships with each other and learn shared interests. Group activities are encouraged but not enforced. Each child has opportunities that are appropriate for their specific level of development. The classroom is designed with children in mind so that all items and materials are easily accessible for them. The furniture is the appropriate size for the children to sit comfortably. Young children have the benefit of mentorship from the older children in their class.

In a Montessori classroom, freedom of movement is encouraged within consistent limits. The environment encourages the children to conform to the rules that are in place. The boundaries are often in place to help the children learn how to respect each other and their environment. As the children progress, they learn from their environment. They learn self-discipline when they learn from their mistakes. Because they are free to choose their activities, children are much more motivated to participate and learn. The children are encouraged to look after their environment and tidy up after themselves. It is easy for them to place items back where they belong when everything has a designated place. Children feel a sense of satisfaction when they complete these tasks independently. Maintaining the classroom is practiced every day, after each activity, helping the children to pick up these healthy habits from a young age. A neat and straightforward environment takes away obstacles—providing a space where children can focus primarily on their learning activities without distraction.

Teachers do not hold expectations of the children, as each child is allowed to develop at their own pace. The teacher guides the children and provides them with the environment and materials they require to learn. Teachers do not get involved in play or learning; instead, they carefully observe each child. They motivate the children to be kind and have respect for one another. The teacher will often express the boundaries of the classroom and encourage each child to follow the rules. There is no end goal to any activity or task that the children undertake, as it is the learning process that is more important than the end result. The children do not feel under pressure to be successful; therefore, they enjoy their activities. They don't work towards an outcome—they work for the experience. The children are motivated to express their creativity and have fun.

Many people favor Montessori education over traditional education, and some believe that Montessori works better. A study published in 2006 by Dr. Angeline Lillard claims that children at 5 years old have higher math and reading skills than those that attend public school. In the same study, they compared 12-year-old Montessori taught children to 12-year-old public school children. The results claimed that math and reading skills were on par by this age, whereas social skills appeared to be more developed in Montessori children of this age (Chen, 2013).

In Montessori, the children choose their own pace, and they are not expected to keep up with one another. They get to take on exciting activities and engage in challenges—allowing them to freely expand their comfort zone and develop a natural interest in broader topics. The children are encouraged to respect each other's learning space, and they learn not to interrupt each other. A Montessori classroom is quiet most of the time because each child is focused entirely on their activity. Children can make visual calculations using concrete materials that they can physically manipulate. Montessori education holds many benefits, but most importantly, they aim to help a child prepare for all aspects of life.

CONCLUSION

Maria Montessori created Montessori education to help children achieve their full potential in all aspects of their life. Montessori's efforts are recognized worldwide by parents and educators. Montessori's education is not just for the classroom. Parents all over the world have successfully implemented Montessori methods in their homes. Montessori promotes and instills independence in children throughout the Four Panes of Development—from birth to adulthood. Parents love the Montessori idea because they get to see it work for themselves. The children are observed throughout all levels of development. A Montessori environment is equipped so that children do not have to ask for help. Instead, they have the tools to figure it out by themselves. A Montessori environment can be set up in all rooms in the house and practiced by all family members.

Montessori methods can work from birth, starting with weaning. It is best to wait until your baby is at least 6 months old before starting the weaning process, as their bodies need to have developed enough to handle solid food. You can begin weaning your baby when they can sit up on their own. Be mindful of what you feed your baby and introduce allergy-risk foods one at a time. Start with blended foods and introduce lumpier foods and finger foods as your child progresses. Encourage your child to drink out of an open cup from the earliest possible age. Provide a water jug and a clear glass so your child can pour their drink by themselves—they learn motor skills and mathematical concepts. Provide a child-sized table and chairs so your child has the freedom of movement and is not restricted to a high chair. Allow your child to eat with you as much as possible, as they will observe you and will mimic your actions. When feeding your baby, provide them with child-sized utensils so they can watch you and learn how to feed themselves. Equipment needed for Montessori weaning includes placemats, mugs, glasses, pitchers, bibs, low table and chairs, clear containers, and a toddler kitchen.

In Montessori, children can engage in real-life activities such as cooking, cleaning, and arts and crafts. Reality is preferred over pretend play, as children have fun learning practical life skills. The children can move around freely and have access to functional materials that serve a purpose. Children are allowed to choose what activities they would like to partake in and have the option of working alone or as a team. The materials present

CONCLUSION | 139

obstacles that the children can work out for themselves. The children are encouraged to engage in activities for the experience rather than a result. Children are not told what to play with; they decide for themselves while being carefully observed by the teacher or parent. A Montessori classroom is a quiet and peaceful environment. The children are encouraged to have respect for one another and to look after their surroundings. Children can tidy up after themselves and put all items away in their dedicated space.

A Montessori playroom is just like a Montessori classroom. All methods are the same, and the environment is straightforward and suitable for the child's size and needs. The children have access to all of their toys and cleaning materials and an area for preparing food. Toys are kept to a minimum and are rotated or changed as a child progresses. The space is open and tidy, and everything has a place. Other rooms such as the nursery or bedroom and the bathroom will have to be adjusted to suit Montessori methods. Consider creating an area in the house that you can dedicate to calming down and thinking. Allow your child to become a part of your day-to-day activities such as cleaning, vacuuming, food preparation, and laundry. Learning these skills early on will help them later on in life.

In the playroom or classroom, most Montessori toys are made from natural materials like wood or metal. They are designed to help children focus, engage, and learn. The materials provide a learning experience and are not just entertainment. They help

140 | CONCLUSION

children to develop their sensory, academic, and practical life skills. There are many Montessori toys to choose from; I have provided a list of my favorites to make it a little easier for you.

The Montessori approach to sleeping includes letting your child sleep on a floor bed in a babyproofed nursery or bedroom. Your child is allowed the freedom to move around the room. They have access to low shelves that hold appropriate toys and books. The space is calm, relaxing, and free of obstruction. When putting your child to bed, leave the room calmly and allow your child to self-soothe. Give your child 5 to 10 minutes to calm down before you go back into the room. You can observe at a distance or through a baby monitor. Your child may get out of bed and find a toy or book to play with, and they may fall asleep where they are playing. As long as your child is comfortable, once they are asleep, try not to disturb them. A Montessori bedroom may include a floor bed, a low shelf, art and decor, a pull-up bar, and a mirror.

It is best to wait until your baby is ready until you start potty training. At around 1 year old, your child may begin to show interest in the potty. When their diapers are dry throughout the day, this is a sign that they are starting to control their bladder muscles. You may be able to introduce underwear once your child has started to dress themselves. Once you feel your child is ready, you can begin training. Throw out all diapers as soon as you start, and try to avoid switching back. Talk your child through every step from pulling down their pants, sitting on the potty, wiping, pulling up their pants, and then washing their hands. Once you've put the potty contents into the toilet, you can allow your child to flush. Make sure your child always has access to their potty throughout the day. When accidents happen, remain calm and let your child help with the clean-up process. When your child's diaper or underwear is wet, change them right away so they appreciate the feeling of being dry. Observe their bowel movements, and set reminders for certain times of the day. Be consistent and stick with it.

In Montessori, there are no rewards or punishments. Children are encouraged to learn self-discipline. Show your child respect using respectful communication. Demonstrate politeness and manners, and your child will follow suit. Try not to get involved in disputes between siblings; allow them to work it out for themselves. Instead of punishing your child when they won't do something you've asked, offer them alternatives and try to figure problems out together. Try not to disturb your child when they are playing and learning, and only offer help when required. Provide a safe and secure environment, and let your child choose their activities. Help them to communicate with others, and explain processes to them as you go along. In your house, set simple boundaries and try to stick to them. Encourage your children to respect the house rules.

There are many benefits to educating and rearing a child using Montessori methods. Children grow a natural love for learning. They work off of instinct and have the tools to develop essential life skills. Montessori children become confident, respectful, independent members of society. This book has provided all of the information required to start implementing Montessori methods today! You can now go ahead and see what works for you and your child. If you enjoyed reading this book, please leave a review on Amazon.

REFERENCES

Age Of Montessori. (n.d.). *A Parent's Introduction to Montessori Materials*. Ageofmontessori.org. Retrieved May 17, 2021, from https://ageofmontessori.org/a-parents-introduction-to-montessori-materials/

American Montessori Society. (n.d.). *Benefits of Montessori Education*. Amshq.org. https://amshq.org/Families/Why-Choose-Montessori/Benefits-of-Montessori#:~:text=Choosing%20a%20Montessori%20environment%20for

Chen, G. (2013, June 6). *Education.com*. Education.com; Education.com. https://www.education.com/magazine/article/10-benefits-montessori-preschool/

Clemer, C. (2018, January 29). *What is Montessori? 10 key principles all parents should know*. Motherly. https://www.

mother.ly/child/what-is-montessori-10-basic-principles-you-need-to-know

Clemer, C. (2020, June 25). *8 Montessori-inspired phrases to use for each stage of potty training.* Motherly. https://www.mother.ly/child/how-to-potty-train-the-montessori-way

Craycroft, M. (2015, September 14). *How to Simply Integrate the Montessori Method at Home.* Carrots Are Orange. https://carrotsareorange.com/how-to-create-a-montessori-at-home-environment/

Did you know your baby will give you 3 signs they're ready for solid foods? Find out more. (n.d.). Start4Life. https://www.nhs.uk/start4life/weaning/ready-or-not/

Fundacion Montessori. (2018). *The Montessori Method.* FAMM. https://www.fundacionmontessori.org/the-montessori-method.htm

Gray, P. (2008, November 19). *The Value of Play I: The Definition of Play Gives Insights.* Psychology Today. https://www.psychologytoday.com/gb/blog/freedom-learn/200811/the-value-play-i-the-definition-play-gives-insights

Hapa Family. (2020, February 20). *MONTESSORI AT HOME: Your Floor Bed Questions ANSWERED!* Www.youtube.com. https://www.youtube.com/watch?v=Z9fHShu8YJ4

How We Montessori. (2019, July 17). *What Montessori Parents Do Differently - Toilet Learning*. How We Montessori. https://www.howwemontessori.com/how-we-montessori/2019/07/what-montessori-parents-do-differently-toilet-learning.html

J&e. (2020, May 9). *How To Childproof Your House For Montessori (With Pictures)*. The Family Pillar. https://thefamilypillar.com/how-to-childproof-your-house-for-montessori-with-pictures/

LeadKid Academy. (2020, October 10). *Montessori Sleep Training & Bedroom Setup*. Medium. https://medium.com/@leadkid/montessori-sleep-training-bedroom-setup-495cc6cf65cb#:~:text=The%20Montessori%20approach%20to%20sleeping

Mead, S. (n.d.). *The History of the Montessori Education*. Www.whitbyschool.org. Retrieved May 11, 2021, from https://www.whitbyschool.org/passionforlearning/the-history-of-the-montessori-education#:~:text=The%20Early%201900s%3A%20-Montessori%20First%20Comes%20to%20America&text=By%201912%2C%20Dr.

Montessori Method. (n.d.). *Montessori Playroom - How To Create A Montessori Play Space At Home*. Montessori Method. https://montessorimethod.com/playroom/#:~:text=Montessori%20Playroom%20Questions-

Montessori Rocks. (2017, May 11). *Sleep Tips for Implementing a Montessori Bedroom for Your Baby or Toddler*. Montessori Rocks. https://montessorirocks.org/sleep-tips-for-implementing-a-montessori-bedroom-for-your-baby-or-toddler/

Monti Kids. (2020, August 13). *What makes a toy a Montessori toy?* Monti Kids. https://montikids.com/montessori/what-makes-toy-montessori/

Our Montessori Home. (2012, September 7). *5 Reasons Why We Chose Montessori*. Ourmontessorihome.com. http://www.ourmontessorihome.com/5-reasons-why-we-chose-montessori/

Preschlack, P. L. (n.d.). *The Four Planes of Development: Child Development in Four Questions*. Retrieved May 11, 2021, from https://forestbluffschool.org/wp-content/uploads/2018/12/The-Four-Planes-of-Development.pdf

Small World. (2018, March 8). *A Montessori Approach to Bedtime: Establishing a Healthy Sleep Routine*. Small World Montessori School. https://swmschool.org/2018/03/08/a-montessori-approach-to-bedtime-establishing-a-healthy-sleep-routine/

Symon, B., Crichton, G., & Muhlhausler, B. (2017). Does the early introduction of solids promote obesity? *Singapore Medical Journal, 58*(11), 626–631. https://doi.org/10.11622/smedj.2017024

The Discovery School of Jacksonville. (2019, July 18). *Montessori At Home: Toddler Potty Training Tips*. Www.youtube.com. https://www.youtube.com/watch?v=GUmsME9l4Dc

The Montessori Notebook. (n.d.). *Receive your free "Instead of this say that" PDF download*. The Montessori Notebook. Retrieved May 25, 2021, from https://www.themontessorinotebook.com/instead-of-this-say-that/

The Montessori Notebook. (2014, May 22). *A Montessori approach to toilet training*. The Montessori Notebook. https://www.themontessorinotebook.com/montessori-approach-toilet-training/

The Montessori Notebook. (2015a, May 18). *How to stop saying "no" forever + what to say instead*. The Montessori Notebook. https://www.themontessorinotebook.com/stop-saying-no-forever/

The Montessori Notebook. (2015b, June 19). *Setting limits Montessori-style*. The Montessori Notebook. https://www.themontessorinotebook.com/setting-limits-montessori-style/

The Montessori Notebook. (2016a, March 6). *Montessori activities at home with toddlers and preschoolers*. The Montessori Notebook. https://www.themontessorinotebook.com/montessori-activities/

The Montessori Notebook. (2016b, June 6). *How to stay calm – the ultimate guide for parents*. The Montessori Notebook. https://www.themontessorinotebook.com/stay-calm/

The Montessori Notebook. (2016c, November 14). *The ultimate list of Montessori activities for babies, toddlers and preschoolers*. The Montessori Notebook. https://www.themontessorinotebook.com/montessori-activities-for-babies-toddlers-and-preschoolers/

The Montessori Notebook. (2017, May 7). *Montessori and pretend play: a complicated question*. The Montessori Notebook. https://www.themontessorinotebook.com/montessori-and-pretend-play/

The Montessori Notebook. (2020, November 16). *A Montessori approach to discipline*. The Montessori Notebook. https://www.themontessorinotebook.com/montessori-approach-to-discipline/

Transparent Watering Can. (n.d.). Montessori Child. Retrieved May 13, 2021, from https://www.montessorichild.com.au/products/clear-watering-can

Wikipedia Contributors. (2019, May 15). *Maria Montessori*. Wikipedia; Wikimedia Foundation. https://en.wikipedia.org/wiki/Maria_Montessori

Woods, N. (2021, February 16). *What is The Best Mattress for a Toddler Floor Bed?* Montessori Up! https://www.montessoriup.com/montessori-mattress/